A Pacific Crest Odyssey

Walking the Trail from Mexico to Canada

David Green

 WILDERNESS PRESS • BERKELEY

Copyright © 1979 by David Green
Cover by Larry Van Dyke
Design by Jeffrey P. Schaffer

Library of Congress Card Catalog Number 79-66298

International Standard Book Number 911824-91-X
Published by Wilderness Press
          2440 Bancroft Way
          Berkeley CA, 94704

For Claudia

who first shared with me the mountains, that I might now
share them with others

Acknowledgements

In a venture as self-involved as a marathon hike, particularly in the telling of the story, it is easy to lose track of the significant others in the experience. A few lines on a single page seem hardly thanks enough.

To the North Face of Berkeley, California, and the Danner Boot Company and Oregon Mountain Community of Portland, Oregon, for their gracious assistance in outfitting the trek, my wallet sends its warmest regards.

For the various homefolk who lightened the emotional load, and particularly the Hassalo Street House — my lifeline to civilization — I've saved my heart.

—David Green
Somes Bar, CA
June 11, 1979

Contents

Southern California 1
The High Sierra 25
The Northern Sierra 45
Northern California 61
Oregon 81
Washington 99
Afterword 119
Appendix A: Menu 121
Appendix B: Equipment 126
Appendix C: Special Logistical Considerations ...139
Index 145

Preface

For three days, the North Cascades had been bathed in a mist so fine that I had been able to look up and see the sky beyond the membranous film of cloud, yet so constant as to provoke illusions of the Flood. The rains ended on the fourth day as I perched atop the plateau north of Whatcom Pass. By evening, the clouds lifted, parted; the heavens were revealed. It was a glorious sight — the awesome expanse of Challenger Glacier funneling into the long, tumultuous cascade of its icefall, the ice-sharpened spines of the North Pickets shredding the horizon — but perhaps the effect of the vision was tempered somewhat by my simple feelings of relief at the break in the weather. For it was not until the next day that I experienced the Moment.

I was walking the valley bottom below Whatcom Pass then, and stopped a while to sit atop a stump amidst the gentle tranquility of the forest. The heady aroma of damp earth, the scent of fecundity, filled the air. There was only that sound that is no sound, but more a presence, soft and ephemeral as an angel's whisper, rhythmic and constant as the heartbeat of the earth. The forest rose around me, towering, welcoming, sheltering, at once giving me the comfort of a mother, the guidance of a mentor. It was a dream, it was magic — the soul is quicker than the eye — and I wished the Moment never to end.

x

I no longer remember for how many days the desire to immortalize the experience of wilderness perfection lay dormant within me. As with the appearance of mushrooms in the forest-deep — existing beneath the surface for untold days before springing up suddenly, overnight, to bulge fully developed above the ground — one day I was sitting behind my office desk, an operative member of society, and the next day I was dreaming of hiking from Mexico to Canada.

The Pacific Crest Trail (PCT) had been making a home for itself in my subconscious for several years. Going to school in Michigan at the turn of the 70s, I was exposed to all the hoopla surrounding Detroiter Erik Ryback's alleged completion of the route from Canada to Mexico in 1971. When I moved to Portland, Oregon, in 1973, I brought myself to within a couple hours' drive of the trail in the northern Oregon Cascades, and became familiar with, and enticed by, its beauty. Too, from National Geographic books to the local paper's near-annual report of some local hiker's experience, the PCT received considerable media coverage. When a whimsical derailment of rational thought sent me in search of a wilderness-forever, the PCT readily suggested itself. Knowing that my contract with a federally funded, educational research project would expire in another year, I was free to pursue the search actively.

Although the trek would take less than six months, the preliminary journey through trail guides and topographic maps, equipment catalogues and nutritional handbooks, the planning and preparation and dreaming and deciding, lasted over a year. The first steps led to the bookstore, to purchase the trail guides. I had been aware of the trail's courses through the Cascades of Oregon and Washington, and that it incorporated the famed John Muir Trail through the High Sierra of California's Sierra Nevada. The trail guides filled in the spaces of my knowledge. They provided the simple grist for my logistical mill: distance, timing, pace, resupply options, obstacles. But they couldn't tell everything. As the months passed, I came to realize that to walk in the mountains for six months would be as much an exploration of the wilderness within myself as of the wilderness around me.

Then the journey of preparation was nearly over, and I found myself lying on a crinkly bed under a spreading live oak tree. The nearby ranch road led to the Mexican border, a chaparral-covered mile to the south. I pulled a fresh notebook from my pack and, by the light of the moon, wrote:

There is a fullish moon tonight, casting shine over the eve of my journey. It is a good time for planting. The walk will grow strong and healthy.

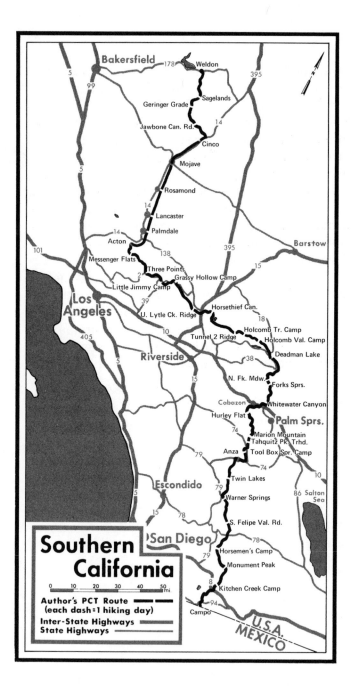

Bakersfield
178
Weldon
5
99
395
Sagelands
Geringer Grade
Jawbone Can. Rd.
14
Cinco
Mojave
Rosamond
14
Lancaster
14
Palmdale
Acton
101
138
Barstow
Messenger Flats
Three Points
395
2
Grassy Hollow Camp
15
Little Jimmy Camp
Los
39
U. Lytle Ck. Ridge
Angeles
Horsethief Can.
18
405
10
Holcomb Tr. Camp
Tunnel 2 Ridge
Holcomb Val. Camp
5
Riverside
38
Deadman Lake
N. Fk. Mdw.
Forks Sprs.
15
Cabazon
Whitewater Canyon
Hurley Flat
Palm Sprs.
74
Marion Mountain
Tahquitz Pk. Trhd.
Anza
Tool Box Spr. Camp
79
74
10
Escondido
Twin Lakes
86 Salton
5
79
Sea
Warner Springs
15
78
S. Felipe Val. Rd.
San Diego
78
79
Horsemen's Camp
Monument Peak
8
Kitchen Creek Camp
94
Campo
U.S.A.
MEXICO

Southern California

| | | |
0 10 20 30 40 50 mi.

Author's PCT Route ▬▬▬
(each dash = 1 hiking day)
Inter-State Highways ▬▬▬
State Highways ▬▬▬

Southern California

Flashback ... "You're going as part of a group?"
"No, I'm going on my own."
"Alone?! Won't you get lonely?"
"Oh, I 'spect I'll meet a few folks along the trail."

*At the Mexican border, alongside an offi-
cial trail marker, is the handmade sign of a
person who completed the trail last year. The
sign wishes Godspeed to future hikers: may
your feet be as strong as your will. It is littered
with the signatures of this year's novitiates: 45
hikers (Trailers) heading for Canada already,
the bulk of them just a day or three ahead of me.
Under the eyes of the resident cattle, I touch
foot and hiking staff beneath the barbed-wire
border and turn northward. Half a mile later, I
meet Trailer number 47. Ah, Dame Solitude,
what a fair and elusive creature thou art.*

From the Mexican border, the route in 1977
was a trail in name only. The first couple hundred
yards pass through two cattle gates and a circular
dirt drive in front of a ranch house and scattered
outbuildings; then it continues down a mile of dirt
road until pavement brings the Trailer into the
town of Campo. For the better part of the first 1½
weeks, wilderness was an italicized concept. The
trail was an incongruous series of lug-sole prints in
the scrabbly shoulders of county highways, vague
boot-etchings in the baked hardpan of old mining
roads and cattlepaths. Trailside companions bore
the stamp of civilization — intermittent fields of
Herefords in kaffee klatsch; the southwestern
gothic of windmill and irrigation pipe; headframes
and related paraphernalia of the short-lived, local
mining boom of a century past, the rusted detritus
of exhausted dreams — evidence of the preponderance of private land that is creating the primary
obstacle to further construction of the permanent
Crest Trail in southern California.

And to this naturalized Oregonian, accustomed
to the volcanic castles and vegetative glut of the

Cascade range, the environs could lay scant claim
to mountainhood. The path follows the northern
extension of the Peninsular Ranges, which origi-
nate in the southern reaches of Baja California, but
the gently contoured, granitic hills of the Laguna
Mountains and the broad expanses of the valleys of
San Felipe, San Jose and Anza projected a horizon-
tal aura. Lowland fields of sage and pastureland,
hillsides of scraggly chaparral, and prickly-pear
outcroppings added further to the flat-earth feel;
the scattered live oaks and occasional cottonwoods
and willows provided slight local relief. Only in the
open forest of Jeffrey pine and black oak on the
heights of the Laguna Mountains, with dwindling,
crusty patches of snow from a recent storm, was
there a hint of the pleasures to come.

*As I wake, the newly waning moon still
rides high above the Laguna Mountains. Over
the desert below is the new day, the first thin
band of rouge. As the sun nears the horizon, the
sky fades, yielding centerstage to slight rib-
bons of cloud whose undersides glow in bur-
nished golds, reflecting off the distant Salton
Sea. Delicate pinks grace the wispy cirrus
fluffs above my head. And now Sol: pinprick
beam flowering into an orb of molten orange.
It is birth, and I play midwife to the morning.*

*Notes from the Center of Bodily Redemp-
tion, or: The Prune Juice, Smoked Oyster and
Mozzarella Cheese Luncheon. Warner Springs
is an afternoon in sensual Nirvanaville,
washing away all bodily ailments, and a lib-
eral coating of trail dust, in the hot mineral
waters of the resort's swimming pools. Now I
know that my color is in some part sun, though*

the mineral waters have de-oiled my skin, etching a fine patina of dryness on my legs.

This is also my first experience meeting up with a collection of Trailers, since many who arrived yesterday are using the hot springs as a layover spot: little Greg, a 15-year old from Seattle attempting to become the youngest to solo from border to border; UC-Irvine students Peter, Pam and Gail, collectors and dispensers extraordinaire *of natural-history tales and trivia; John, from Arizona, failing in his attempt to come to terms with his 85-pound pack; Barry and Mike, marathon runners from the southern California beaches, and their companion, Steve, a Portlander I had briefly met once before. There is an instant camaraderie, of the sort that existed between VW owners in the early 60's, when total strangers would honk and wave at each other.*

Reflections at a midday siesta:
Public flogging! My powers of observation and creative problem solving are not up to crack. Once again this morning a lack of trail markings has me befuddled. Oregon had spoiled me: Labeled trail markers with relatively accurate mileages did little to prepare me for through-trails ending before term in a maze of dirt roads. Too, it is a matter of concentration. When I'm cranked into cruising speed, I lose myself in what a Jack Kerouac character once called "the meditation of the trail," oblivious to the finer details of pace and obtuse trail markings.

Greens! I can't believe it . . . fresh greens! I have them with lunch today for the first time.

After five days, my alfalfa sprouts have come to maturity. Damn near eat half the quart container straight. Fresh, crunchy greens – my, oh my!

Warner Springs was my entry into the Parade. The following night I found myself camped at an obscure little polluted cow puddle, the only public water in a stretch of thirty miles. Nine other Trailers shared the night with me. One by one by twos and threes, the staggered procession pulled out the next morning to leapfrog through the day and gather again in the evening. There was yet a certain charm in the companionship, bartering tales of our first week to enhance the novelty of the venture.

What a beauty! Up out of the hazy, windy broil of Anza Valley. Up through the manzanita and scrub oak and occasional pinyon pine, along the sinuous ridge road of Thomas Mountain. To gently come to rest in the cool, birdsong-laden grove of Jeffrey pines that is the Tool Box Spring Camp. Jeffrey pine has fast become my favorite tree, with the scent of butterscotch exuding from its trunk, its great puffballs of needles, and bark that looks like a jigsaw puzzle of a two-color topo map.

I can't wait for summer to come. Not because it will be warmer. Who needs warmer? ... one Trailer recorded a sun temperature of 118° in the San Felipe Valley a couple of days back. No, it's just that the nights now are too bloody long.

Last night. I bed down with the sun, around 7:30 by a fellow-Trailer's watch. When I awake it is still dark. As I feel fully rested and

*the eastern horizon appears to be lightening, I
prepare for an early start, breakfasting in bed.
When there is no apparent progress in the
morning light, and with the food groggying
me, I return to sleep. To awake the next time to
the moon, several days into wane, just beginning its rise. Hell, it can't be more 'n three in the
morning. That means . . .aaaaaaaarrrrggh, I
ate my breakfast for a midnight snack.*

I did not carry a watch on the walk. One less bar-
rier between the wilderness and myself, I figured.
Even these city-eyes could read the sun well
enough to gauge midday and a few hours to either
side of it. By the time the sun failed to make a
morning appointment, I was over a month into the
journey and had gained a sense of my pace sufficient to measure my days.

In April, however, the nights were still holding
forth for eleven hours or so. For a city-body accustomed to six or seven hours sleep yet taking the
sunset as a soporific, there was many a dark
awakening. I quickly learned that, away from the
glare of citylights, all horizons show lighter than
the heavens overhead; hence I rejected the guidance of this false prophet. But I missed the
quick-fix of a luminescent dial. There is something about waking up to measureless night that
keeps me awake thinking about it.

Eventually, however, I learned to use the far
edge of the Big Dipper's bowl as a two-hour hand as
it made its nightly, counter-clockwise rotation
around the North Star. I could not ask for a more
luminescent dial.

*I find it damned annoying when my body
betrays me, but am beyond words when my
negligence returns the favor. At first there was*

*just a twinge as I went bounding packless up
the side road to the Thomas Mountain summit.
A twinge in that hunk of climbing muscle just
above the knee. Little twinges happen all the
time and I simply ignored it. Now, after eight
miles of descent under pack, I'm faced with a
throbbing, swollen mound of tension that feels
as though my whole thigh has just been to the
dentist.*

There had been several months of yoga afternoons and hill running in Portland parks. Occasional mornings found me stomping around the
winter-fogged neighborhood wearing my old frame
pack filled with fifty pounds of firewood. But all
one can do for his/her body in the city is introduce it
to the syllabus. The learning can come only from
the trail.

To this point my body had been absorbing its
lessons well; the city-briefing had been intensive.
Perhaps I had begun to take it for granted, to turn
my ears to the early morning breezes stirring the
cedar and pine atop Thomas Mountain rather than
listening to the whimper of a body abused. But the
Unheeding have a penalty to pay. It would be more
than three weeks before I would be able to walk
again without first binding the thigh in an outsized
Ace bandage.

*Today has been long – twelve hours on the
trail. It has been arduous – climbing 3400 feet
in 4½ miles, struggling across Tahquitz'
boulder-strewn summit ridge and through
snowfields that would sometimes support
weight, sometimes yield to grab and claw the
thigh. The day has ended in hastening darkness, fourteen miles farther and 3200 feet
higher than it began, in a small, snow-*

bedecked, waterless meadow on Marion Mountain's shoulder. Melting snow under the star-packed awning, while wet feet chill and thigh muscle-strain begs mercy. Eating a gritty noodles romanoff in warming mummybag . . . warming sleep.

It has been a stunning day, though: the snowy sheerness of Tahquitz Peak's north face as it plummets 2400 feet to Strawberry Valley . . . the sun-cleaned slopes of Marion Mountain and Jean Peak as they ease into a similar plunge from their 10,000-foot heights . . . the subalpine meadow delicacy of Strawberry Cienega, this last when sensitivities had been dulled by nearly 11 hours on the trail.

After 1½ weeks on the docile treadmill of the southern California hills, the trail had wound its way up into the high country of the San Jacinto Mountains, a small nest of 10,000-foot peaks cradling the imposing summit of 10,804-foot Mt. San Jacinto. The snowbound trail provided a grueling challenge for a body of now-questionable hardiness, while slaking the thirst of a parched spirit.

Southern California is so starved for wildlands that this diminutive mountain park of conifer and granite spires houses both state and federally designated wilderness areas. Yet the San Jacintos cannot escape the long arm of their southern California environs.

What an abomination! Lying here beneath the spreading shelter of a giant pine, gazing up at a stars-stricken sky, and what should I see but a spotlight sweep. Looks like it probably originates in Palm Springs. Leave it to the city

*folk to louse up a perfectly wonder-full night-
light show with their electric toys.*

*Damnedest thing! At 8800 feet, on a trail
leading up to a 10,800-foot summit, the graffiti
in the purgehouse at the Deer Springs Trail
Camp talked of little but surfing and
skateboarding. Tube it! I'm stoked! Yeehaa!
All the more incongruous on a frigid morning
with 2-3 feet of snowpack underfoot.*

*Good God, San Gorgonio Mountain has
disappeared. Making like Alice's cheshire cat,
it has gradually faded away into the smog. An
11,500-foot mountain quietly devoured by the
auto.*

The smog rose up out of the freeway-filled pit of
San Gorgonio Pass, better known as the major
arterial connecting Los Angeles with Palm
Springs than as the low point of the Crest Trail in
California at 1185 feet. Sinkhole of mechanized
society that it is, the Pass is nevertheless topog-
raphically striking: a yawning, 7000-foot chasm
between the towering peaks of the San Jacinto
Mountains to the south and the San Bernardino
Mountains to the north.

After the previous afternoon's bloody
snowwhacking and the chaparral-bushwhacking
exit from the San Jacintos, I spent an afternoon
recuperating in the sultry desert heat of San Gorgonio Pass. Then I ascended up through the sandy
reaches of cactus, chia and chaparral in Whitewater Canyon, up the spinning thread of Mission
Creek into the welcoming pine- and cedar-scented
arms of the San Bernadino high country.

*Climbing up the ridge above Whitewater
Canyon I am intrigued by the proliferation of a*

*particular flowering plant: velvet golf ball of
rippling maroon ridges and lime valleys, with
miniscule lavender flowers spattered ran-
domly across the surface of the sphere. I ask
Peter about it. "Oh, that's the chia plant," he
exclaims. "Here, let me show you." He looks
about until he finds a shriveled ball of brown
and crushes it between his fingers. Sure
enough, there are a dozen or so of those little,
gelatinous black seeds, $2.40 a pound in your
local natural food store, lying in his palm. Gail
chimes in with the tale that one mouthful of
chia seeds is said to have sustained an Indian
warrior through a full day's forced march. The
lesson ended, we continue on up the ridge.*

Knowledge of wilderness vegetation has always been one of those desirables, like the ability
to overhaul a car engine or make my own clothes,
that I wish to have spring, fully developed, into my
magic bag of tricks without my having to undergo
the long, often laborious, discovery process that is
Learning. But the mountains have usually been
for me an occasional explosive weekend of city-
escape. No space was ever made for the ponderous,
pondering investigation of the vegetable world
through which I walked. Natural-history books of
every flavor and hue, bought in a fit of impulse,
gathered dust on my shelves.

Six months of mountaining will be the perfect
opportunity for such discovery, I had thought re-
peatedly during the months of planning. But provisions for self-sufficiency filled all the corners of
my pack. The magnitude of all I wanted to learn
would weigh too heavily on my back. For it was a
comprehensive body of knowledge that I dreamed
of possessing, which precluded a selective process.

Rather than carry a single guide to trees, wildflowers or geology, I left them all to their dust-
gathering. I would be nearly two months into the
journey before recognizing my need for movement
in the mind as well as in the body and finally
adding a natural-history field guide to my pack.

*Clean at last! Clean at last! Great God Al-
mighty, I'm clean at last.*
*And it is so fine. Like a breath of Eden after
the veritable cauldron of the San Bernardino
foothills. Layers of coolness in the tiny pond.
Turn a flip and I pass through the entire range
of thermal sensation. Grime-bejeweled pores
spit out their costuming and I come out of the
pond in clean wrapping. The newborn babe
then walks with his friends, through licorice
marble-cake rock, up the canyon of Mission
Creek to camp.*

The Bad Water Blues:
I got the Bad Water Blues,
The Bad Water Blues, I'm tol'.
I got the Bad Water Blues,
The Bad Water Blues, that's so.
Well, my grits slip through my system . . .
Like they slidin' down a greased flagpole.

The outriders of civilization came quickly to the
edge of the wilderness. Huge yellow Cats, with
paws of rubber tread and hearts of steel piston and
cylinder, had clawed new paths in the forest.
Polished dwellings of cedar and glass, monuments
erected to the Protestant Ethic and city-prowess,
dotted my path as I drifted down to the summer
resort of Big Bear Lake.

The high peaks of the San Gorgonio Wilderness
receded in the southern haze as I climbed up from a
day of laundering and fresh food feasting to begin a

westward traverse of the San Bernardino and San Gabriel Mountains. These ranges were the only east-west trending mountain ranges along the entire journey. Nine days were spent treading their heterogeneous mix of man and mountain, reflecting the influence of the Los Angeles megalopolis to the southwest and the Mojave Desert to the north. The San Bernardinos were the more gentle country, the more greatly tamed: small ranches and campgrounds tucked into niches in the pine-coated crest; the semi-arid slopes spotted with clumps of rural folk and orchards; "temporary trail" on state highway winding through the desert lowlands, connecting the massive evaporation pools — Big Bear Lake, Lake Arrowhead, Silverwood Lake — of southern California's reservoir system.

The San Gabriels are separated from the San Bernardinos by the great gash of the San Andreas Fault, which bisects the ranges near Cajon Canyon. Crossing the fault in adjacent Lone Pine Canyon, the trail quickly regained the heights, twining its path with dirt-bike trails and the Angeles Crest Highway. Whereas the roadways followed the gradient of least resistance, the trail wandered up the snow-packed slopes of 9399-foot Mt. Baden-Powell, with its ancient limber-pine groves, and dropped down into the slender canyon of Little Rock Creek. I continued westward to within a ridge or two of the Los Angeles basin, whose ubiquitous smog created splendid sunsets and is causing extensive needle damage to the mountain forests, before turning north to descend into the Mojave Desert.

Washed my clothes yesterday, their first laundering in three weeks. My body, on the other hand, remains a stinking, grimy sculpture, crafted from trail dust and sun. My trail coating is worn as a badge . . . perhaps as a suit of armor.

However pleasant the feeling of being clean, I found it of little use on the trail. There is no overestimating the desiccation that results from 24-hour exposure to mountain air. When watered, my skin did not thrive, it molted. While some Trailers carried moisturizing soap and lotions in their gear, I chose principally to ignore the whole issue. Though self-consciously filthy while passing through the occasional oases of civilization, I melted right in to the earthiness of the trail. This way too, I rarely had to overcome the Dirty Fingernail Syndrome, that creeping feeling of "getting dirty" that the Clean Person experiences upon entering the mountains.

The San Bernardinos wear a thin overcast this morning, making two dimensions of everything. My energy too is two-dimensional as I slog listlessly through the sandy trail. Then a rustle, and two deer burst from a thicket on my right. I settle to a stop, as do they . . . pause, immobile. There is not a breath of movement in the air. Then they move on, as do I . . . much more like the deer now.

Alone. For the first time in two weeks, I slept alone and woke not knowing when I would see my next Trailer. Oh, I know they are there, before me and behind. But for now I'm alone, like driving down a foggy highway, just me and my small sphere of clarity.

There was only one person I had full seriously invited to join me on this journey, an old college chum who was the only person in my mountaining past with whom I had felt I had enough personal space. It is a rare art, rarely practiced, for members of a group to allow each other the sanctity of the individual. Yet even as the invite flew off to Elliot, my heart had been planning the trek as a solo venture. When he had written that he would be unable to join me, I had been relieved. I wanted the flexibility to choose companionship or solitude as my whim directed.

But after nearly three weeks on the trail amidst the crush of the Trailer horde, I had hiked alone only two days, slept alone but three nights. I tired of the company: the pressuring exuberance of their youth, like that of a playful pup; the endless discussions of equipment, that inevitable common denominator of the trail. I expected the convention-center ambience to diminish in the abundantly-watered Sierra, where pace and daily destination wouldn't be as uniformly dictated by Mother E's arid hand at the tap. But I couldn't shake the sense of foreboding. If the company of Trailers was a burden, what of summer and vacationers. I could see my epitaph:

Here lies David,
Buried under a mountain of weekenders:
Three miles and a cloud of campfire smoke.

Good God, the ten pounds I gained for this trip are gone already. I see myself in a big mirror at Silverwood Lake and the ribs are right out there. Gad, the body fat was supposed to last me into the Sierra.

Months of running and my borderline-vegetarian diet had created a slim city-body. To aid the transition to my trail diet, and to provide a little extra insulation against the Sierran chill in the second month of the trek, I had gained ten or

twelve pounds of Grade A., US prime fat in the last
weeks before leaving. And I had planned a seemingly excessive, high-carbohydrate diet of about
3500 calories a day. Yet the fat had disappeared
inside of three weeks, leaving me with a growing
feeling of running-on-empty which would continue
to plague me throughout the trek.

I had two immediate reactions to my condition
of insatiability. The first was to take every advantage of the trail's outposts of civilization to ingest
meals that would rival those of Diamond Jim
Brady. Positively obscene masses of food would
pass through my ravenous maw, to swell and
gurgle in my innards, producing spells of flatu-
lence that could kill a deer at a hundred paces.
During the course of the journey I would spend
nearly double the $400 I had alloted for town food
and emergencies ... and there never were any
emergencies.

My second response was an unwilling en-
dorsement of the sugar industry. I had been born
with a sweet tooth but had managed to cap it during recent years. Although I had retained a weak-
ness for good ice cream, my annual intake of soda
and candy bars could be tallied on the digits of a
two-toed sloth. By the end of the first month of the
walk, however, every one-horse, gas station-
grocery or lakeside resort would see me hitting up
a quick fix of 2000-3000 calories of junk. My
natural-food friends would be mortified; my pan-
creas probably was.

*To make up for the ignominy of having a
wilderness trail pass through a cement culvert
underneath an interstate expressway, the new
section of Crest trail rising from Cajon Canyon and I-15 is routed through a small desert*

arboretum. Signs identify cottonwood, yerba santa, cane cholla and similar vegetation which I had seen as no more than obscure, knee-high foliage till now. A touch of class in a tiny corner of the expressway's backyard. Even a rattlesnake for a doorman.

I've been watching lizards lately. You know, when pronounced in a certain way, their name is a bit onomatopoeic. Say "Lits'rt" and watch the little buggers skitter about as you approach. Quite apt, don't you think?

It's been a long day, as the day over Tahquitz Peak was long. This time, however, there was no screaming thigh muscle, no anxiety over what was happening, what might happen. There was only the mountain, its demands and its gifts, and myself, my abilities and my rewards. Oftentimes, my concentration was so intense that I was unaware of how much time had passed, how much ground had been covered. Then a moment of relaxation, and my stomach would howl, the sun and mountains juxtaposed differently from last time I had noticed. Accomplishment is painted in many different colors.

My walking staff has become a full-fledged appendage. At the apex of the Mt. Williamson trail, I drop my gear to stroll up the ¼-mile summit path. It isn't twenty paces, however, before I realize my stride feels somehow unnatural. The staff has become the percussion section in my mountain movement.

Little Rock Creek is a dream. In the past 3½ days, there have been just two sources of water and they were both posted unsafe for drinking.

To come upon a creek, rushing water over fallen logs, a bit of a waterfall settling in a granite punchbowl pool . . . to come upon moss, for God's sake! Ah, bliss . . . may I never move from this site. The thigh muscle is in agreement; it got a bit overexcited at the sight of all that water and has come down with a slight case of indigestion.

As I round the bend, I can see the fog in the distance, oozing down the slope I am to cross, pillowing up in the valley bottom. A shallow fog; I can see the ridgetop across the way. The recent sunset pinkens its sky-edge. As I near the fog, I can smell the wet, like laundry fresh out of the washer. And as I enter, it crinkles my edges with chill.

The Pacific Crest Trail is meant to be a mountain trail. To skirt the western edge of the Mojave Desert, the proposed permanent Crest Trail would follow a circuitous route through the Sawmill, Liebre and Tehachapi Mountains to bring it into the southern reaches of the Sierra Nevada. But much of this hill country remains outside the public domain, and the inability to obtain easements on private land continues to frustrate trail construction. The temporary trail was forced down onto the desert floor, where the continuing frustration for the Trailer in southern California — the lack of accessible water — became a more serious consideration.

In the San Gabriels there had been late-season snowpack to melt down for supper water, supplementing the up-to-1½ gallons I carried; the Mojave would not be so accommodating. Granted, the western Mojave is high desert, between 2000 and 3000 feet in elevation, and it was yet early spring

— how could there possibly be any harm in a countryside abloom with the delicate pinks and yellows, the rich rouges, of prickly pear and cholla? Still and all, one needed to be pretty highly motivated to carry the twenty-five pounds of water that one long waterless stretch of the suggested temporary trail required. And I had become a bit jaded by the relative barrenness of the southern California terrain. I saw this desert leg as a final indignity to be suffered before reaching the mecca of the High Sierra.

In order to minimize the insult, the temporary trail's 105 miles of mixed dirt and paved backroads were rejected in favor of 45 miles of the Old Sierra Highway, passing through the small towns of Palmdale, Lancaster, Rosamond and Mojave. It was no more than a morning's walk between towns, allowing for shady siestas and shameful displays of gluttony during the heat of the day. A windfall week of lone hiking had come to an end in Acton, the desert's doorstep, as I played adopted son to a local family for a day. Then the misery of roadwalking was shared with two southern Californians, Rick and Fred, who felt no more at home in this desolate corner of their backyard than I.

The desert proved to be a surprisingly sympathetic host, though. Breezy-chill dawns kept me in my wools till mid-morning, and sixty miles-an-hour dinner winds in the town of Mojave took my spirit for an evening walk to a High Sierran pass. And my return to the hill country a few days later brought even more surprising gifts.

Let me introduce you to a dried prune. An excellent backpacking companion, with its half-sweet chewiness, its quality of note is the pit. The pit, you cry, how so?

The prune pit, when held in the mouth and tossed between tongue and cheek, is an anti-desiccant without peer. Why, with a prune pit and a little chapstick, I can just about fool my mouth into thinking I'm sitting down to a quart of Bob's finestkind ice cream, while the waterless miles melt beneath my boots.

The desert environment requires microcosmic vision, a major shift from the macrocosmic focus that suits me so well in the mountains. To look closely, however, is to move slowly and my druthers are to get on down the road. So I keep my large eyes in, seeing the skittering of lizards, an occasional Satan's slither in the sand, and the Joshua tree, a vegetative orangutan unique to the southern California high deserts. And the 5000-foot ridges of the Piute Mountain foothills rising two days to the north — my escape from the desert.

On the eighth day is the resurrection.

The hills are quilted with dirtbike trails. But they are hills. Which will grow into ridges and valleys. Soon to become mountains, the Piutes, with named peaks: Butterbredt, Sorrell, Nicolls.

Seven days did he reside with the heathen, below 3000 feet. On the eighth day he returns to the mountains and the kingdom of heaven.

Mountain storms mind no keeper. Storm-sitting then becomes a true expression of diurnalism. The storm-sitter eats and sleeps. Perhaps reads a bit or writes some letters if it is daylight, or ponders the nature of the cosmos and reflects on women he's known and loved if it is dark. And eats and sleeps some more.

Time is civilization's toy.

There is an undertone of quiet joy to the journey. Yet there are moments when a more intense emotional expression surfaces, such as the early evening break in the storm after 24 hours of snow and rain, and more snow. With unabashed exultation, we whoop and holler about as the sunset gilds the snow-laced trees around us and the hills across the valley burst into the flames of evening-light.

Ah, but emotions, like the weather, are ephemeral creatures. The return of the storm an hour later is greeted with stoic acceptance.

A small going-away present from Old Man Winter, spasmodic in his attention to duties this past year, due to the senility of old age perhaps. Seven inches of snow under a clinging mop of grey, but still for a moment. By midday, we've waded through close to a foot of new snow with our increasing elevation, and there's more of both in our path. Discretion knocks us up aside the head and we hike out a side route, through gentle sheets of quickly falling snow that dance images on the eye like phosphenes, to the protective low elevations of Kelso Valley.

Another day of valley walking brought us into Weldon, the trail's final supply stop before climbing into the High Sierra. The late-season storm had wreaked havoc with the relative gentility of the journey. We had fought a mere skirmish with the weather in the Piutes. Trailers already in the High Sierra had been embattled for several days, receiving up to three feet of new snow. Trailer Central in Weldon was the KOA campground, a-swarm with displaced persons and tales of snow-siege and retreat. Some Trailers had been in resi-

dence for nearly a week, waiting for the weather to
break. Others, too antsy to sit in our dusty,
spotlight-and-swimming-pool encampment, hitch-
hiked north to Mammoth, Yosemite, even
Lake Tahoe, in an attempt to get above the storm.
As a newcomer with fresh supplies to process and a
stringy body to fatten, I was not immediately im-
patient with my tawdry surroundings. There was
nothing for it but to sit back and wait for the
weather to mend.

Trail Log

Despite the existence of a trail guide giving
mileages to the nearest tenth of a mile, compiling
an accurate trail log for the PCT is an impossible
undertaking. Particularly in southern California,
where so much of the trail is in the ongoing process
of being built, the guide's information sometimes
simply did not jibe with reality. Then there were
the occasional detours: skirting the Cahuilla Indian Reservation outside Anza; following the Old
Sierra Highway in the Mojave Desert. Too, day's
end did not always coincide with the mileage
landmarks of the guide. A particularly absurd
example of this was my cool-of-the-evening walk
up the new section of trail climbing out of Lone
Pine Canyon, which ended with my sleeping directly on the narrow trail cut into the slopes of
Upper Lytle Creek Ridge. Nevertheless, given the
margin of error I've allowed myself by rounding off
each day's mileage to the nearest mile, I believe the
figures recorded here are reasonably accurate. I

have noted with an asterisk those cases in which there was nothing for it but to pull a number out of the hat.

Elevations of my evening camps are included for those of you who are detail-freaks like myself. For the same reasons as above, preciseness was elusive. After all, who cares what the elevation of Palmdale is except the manufacturers of city-limit signs. Again, asterisks note the more uncertain entries, which are estimated at the nearest 100 feet. All other elevations have been rounded off to the nearest ten feet.

Southern California Trail Log

Date	Camp	Elevation	Mileage
April 4	Kitchen Creek Camp	3820	14
5	Monument Peak	6270	15
6	Horsemen's Group Camp	4710	17
7	San Felipe Valley Road	3050	20
8	Warner Springs	3130	11
9	Lower Twin Lake	4080	17
10	Anza — supply pick-up	3920	17
11	Tool Box Spring Camp	6150	10
12	Tahquitz Peak South Ridge Trailhead	5440	15
13-14	Marion Mountain's west shoulder — layover day	8640	14
15	Hurley Flat	3450	14
16	Whitewater Canyon	1500*	15
17	Forks Springs area	4800	19
18	North Fork Meadow area	6840	7
19	Deadman Lake	7240	17
20	Holcomb Valley campground — supply pick-up in Big Bear City	7350	12
21	Holcomb Trail Camp	5220	15
22	Tunnel 2 Ridge	5500*	16
23	Horsethief Canyon area	3680	15
24	Upper Lytle Creek Ridge	4500*	15*
25	Grassy Hollow Campground	7320	19*
26	Little Jimmy Campground	7430	11
27	Three Points	5910	19
28	Messenger Flats	5840	24
29-30	Acton — supply pick-up/ lay-over day	2700	15
May 1	Palmdale area	2700*	12
2	Lancaster area	2400*	9
3	Rosamond area	2300*	12
4	Mojave	2780	13
5	Cinco	2140	17
6	Jawbone Canyon Road	4300*	14
7-8	Geringer Grade — layover day	6250	13
9	Kelso Valley at Sagelands	4000	15*
10-14	Weldon — supply pickup/layover	2630	20

Totals
508 miles
34 hiking days
7 layover days

High Sierra

0 10 20 30 40 mi.

Author's PCT Route
Inter-State Highways
State Highways

YOSEMITE

Mono Lake

NEVADA
CALIFORNIA

Tuolumne Meadows
120

Yosemite Valley

NAT.

49

140

Donohue Pass

49   41

PARK

Shadow Lake

Reds Meadow
DEVILS POST.
NAT. MON.

Mammoth
Lakes
Old Mammoth

Duck Pass

Silver Pass

6

L. Edison

395

Sally Keyes Lks.

McClure Mdw.

Bishop

KINGS

Muir Pass

Palisades Creek

Fresno

S. Fk. Kings R.

180

CANYON

Woods Creek

99

180

63

N.P.

245

Bubbs Creek

SEQUOIA

Tyndall Creek

Visalia

198

Wallace Creek

N.P.

Guitar Lake
MT. WHITNEY

Kern Hot Sprs.

Crabtree R.S.

Lone Pine

Soda Springs

Grasshopper Flat

190

Kern Flat

Fks. of Kern

65

395

Brush Creek

Ant Canyon

99

155

Bull Run Ck.

Lake Isabella

Bakersfield

178

Weldon

58

14

The High Sierra

Grey days and greyer dispositions. A daily influx of Trailers built up behind the weather-narrowed bottleneck of Weldon: after three days I had two dozen campmates, all waiting for the same moment of sun-blessed departure. Inertia set in, and a numbing ambivalence. After several weeks in Sol's company, with warm earth under foot for the most part, I wasn't eager to slog through the chilling molasses of knee-high fresh snow. And after the last three weeks of taking companions only when my fancy led me to, I was not willing to be party to the growing Weldon Expeditionary Force.

Too, there was the matter of the 85-pound pack. The Crest Trail would lead over 260 miles before reaching the next on-trail supply point. There are accessible intermediate towns, but they all lie miles off the trail, and thousands of feet below it. To take advantage of this opportunity for extended wilderness isolation, I would be carrying food for 22 days. Accustomed to carrying but a seven-to-ten day supply and the more sensible burden of 45-55 pounds, I did not approach this weightier task with any great eagerness.

Snow, crowds, weight. With all these new variables, I felt like I was starting from scratch, and I was awash with the insecurity of a new venture. When Rick invited me to be part of a foursome taking an alternate route up the Kern River Canyon, I quickly accepted. The Kern River lies several miles west of the still-temporary route of the Crest Trail, paralleling its northward climb into the High Sierra. However, unlike the designated trail, which makes an immediate climb out of Weldon to the then-snowy elevations of 7000-8000 feet, the Kern River Trail would be a gentle ascent. It would be over a week before we reached snow-country; a leisurely week to eat down into our hefty packs, to escape from the mass of Trailer-humanity. Besides, I had a certain affinity for this trio I was joining. Although of dissimilar backgrounds — Rick was an off-duty news reporter for a Los Angeles television station, Fred and Mike were Forest Service firefighters from San Diego and Mt. Laguna, and I was coming off three years of educational research — our age range of 26-28 years put us in the "Geritol Generation" of the Trailer community. With very few exceptions, most notably a 55-year-old man from Colorado, Trailers could still claim sharp recollections of pubescence.

I have known for several months that I would be heading into the High Sierra, for three weeks on the John Muir Trail, with 80 to 90 pounds on my back – 80, 90 . . . just numbers on a piece of paper. To carry that much weight is incomprehensible.

Was incomprehensible. My hips feel as though they've been set in hot coals, my shoulders and ribs clamped in a vise, my feet as though I've been walking rocky river bottoms barefoot. But after five days of Weldontown malaise, I sleep at trailside with Bull Run Creek rushing by my head and God turning on his streetlamps. My spirit is warm and loose from its day of massage.

The forced immobility in Weldon had been a
small death. The KOA campground had a pocket
business complex: store, laundry room, rec room.
During the first few days there, when the storm
was passing through old age with a bit of spittin'
and pissin', I would walk into the rec room and find
the walls papered with Trailers — sewing ragged
clothing, reading dog-eared magazines, shooting
pool, playing pinball. It was like walking into the
dayroom of "One Flew Over the Cuckoo's Nest."
Life and sparkle were gradually swallowed up, extinct species in the LaBrean tarpits of ennui. One
Trailer, whom I'd met up with several times earlier
but had not seen for over three weeks, arrived in
Weldon two days after I did. He remarked that he
had never seen me before without a smile.

At the journey's beginning, I had expected to be
swept away by the spirit of adventure, riding the
wilderness roller coaster between manic depression and orgiastic thrills of unbounded ecstasy.
Instead, I found myself placidly adapting to the
rhythm of the trail. Awakening with Sol's first
knock on night's door . . . swinging my existence up
onto my back, to move sensually through the day.
Eating when hungry, obeying the dictates of body-
time rather than clocktime. Ending each day a
willing captive of the heathen Sandman. The trail
had become my life, my sustenance, my joy.

My trail mantra is mmmmmmmm-
mooooooooooonnnths. With six months to work
with, what difference does it make if I push to
top that ridge an hour sooner? Lighten up a
tad, and I can smell the sagebrush rather than
the acrid stench of reheated sweat. Take the
time to explore Packsaddle Cave, a massive
Tom-and-Becky honeycomb of caverns and
crawl spaces. The body has a better sense of
purpose than does the mind.

The borrowed fishing pole is unfamiliar in my hands; I am just beginning to reel in when it strikes. After a false start, instinct keeps me reeling in. Moments later, some seven inches of rainbow wriggles breathlessly on the bank . . . my first fish. A bit scared by the little critter's energy, I gingerly remove the hook, then run wide-eyed back to camp, holding my prize out in front of me. Into a pot of water, makeshift creel, and I return to my river. One strike and no rewards later, I'm back at camp. To clean the bit of catch and cook it over the fire, skewered on a green forked stick like a marshmellow. Food of the gods, the skin crackles like rice paper as I suck the tender flesh from the bone, feeding on the magic that brings folk to the river.

This morning I hike through a tree graveyard – a monument to man. According to the bikers we met yesterday, the fire of three years ago that created this forest of shadowy skeletons was started by a backpacker. Our companion, Mike, who had helped fight the blaze, had heard it then attributed to the bikers who reign over this small section of designated bike trails along the Kern River. Whichever bias is your personal god, the hillsides of slender tombstones, the smell of death, remain. As with many of man's creations, there is an unlikely beauty to this stark black forest in the early morning light.

As I enter the long, grassy stretch of Trout Meadow, it is mine. I am alone for the moment and it mirrors the solitude: its isolated spa-

ciousness, flanked by high wooded ridges; the lone glacial erratic, a lodestone in the middle of this plain. I stretch naked to the sun on the grainy, lichened surface of the rock, and take communion with my spirit.

The petroleum stench, the grating howl of the machine, the ugly gash in a sodden trail, the campsites defiled by broken glass and semi-charred cans, the staccato pecking of target shooting. What an abomination is the presence of dirt bikes in the wilderness . . . and how opulent their larder, eh?

It began with Mike's discovery of the two-quart canteen of whiskey, bounced off a bike that had passed shortly before. Pouring off a quart, Mike continued on, pondering his preoccupation with food of late. By evening he had decided to go on a fast, a rite of purification after several days in excess. Rather than simply garbage-can the remaining short pint, Mike disappeared into the riverdark to attempt to barter, whiskey for butter, with a neighboring biker encampment. He returned crying "the fast is over, the fast is over," and setting before us bread, hot dogs, link sausage, Spam, potato chips, and a gallon pot of home-made mulligan stew, still hot from the fire. Oh, and a quarter-pound of margarine.

Morning finds us engorged to the point of obscenity. Mike returns to the biker camp with their cookpot. Back he comes, this time with saltines, peanut butter and jelly, more chips, more hot dogs, cornmeal, more margarine. The bikers had already gone, leaving an entire picnic table covered with food, and other bikers scavenging amongst the canned goods. An as-

*tonishing display of conspicuous consumption
and mindless excess. Ah, but the full belly has
no conscience.*

*What better way to celebrate the completion
of seven weeks on the trail than with a hot bath,
courtesy of the National Park Service. Kern
Hot Springs is just a bit of a thing, not more
than a seep really, which the Park Service has
made functional by sinking a pipe into the
slope and running it into a one-and-a-half-
person, algaed concrete tub. It comes equipped
with a wooden modesty panel on three sides
and the Kern River making merry on the
fourth. And, of course, the customary
several-thousand-foot rock walls to the east
and west, a standard feature with all our Kern
Canyon view lots. Aaaaahh, must be jelly
'cause muscles don't shake like that.*

*The deer tracks of the past few days are
filled for our morning eyes. Three young male
deer come to graze the small grassy stretch by
the hot springs. For the most part at ease, they
occasionally spook each other, darting off a
pace or two before settling. Two groups of ani-
mals breakfasting together, one on grass, the
other on hot cereal.*

Our journey up the Kern River had begun amid
the power stations, aqueduct pipelines, fishing resorts and packhorse ranches that line the lower
Kern near its premature demise at man-made
Lake Isabella. As the days passed, the surroundings gave evidence of our gradually increasing elevation and remove. Sage and chaparral had given
way to scattered stands of oak and Coulter pine,
then manzanita, white fir, and Jeffrey and pon-
derosa pine, and finally lodgepole and silver pine.

Man's presence became little more than an occasional derelict stockgate across the trail. Even the shape of the canyon underwent a transformation. Initially a sprawling scene of ill-defined dimensions, it slowly drew itself together, gathering itself up into the classic U-shape designed by the great valley glaciers of millenia past. Finally, a stiff climb through the manzanita- and heather-flecked talus slopes beside Wallace Creek brought us up to a junction with the John Muir Trail, a permanent section of the Crest Trail, and the High Sierra.

The High Sierra . . . the Range of Light. All through the months of planning and dreaming, these were the mountains of magic. Mt. Whitney, at 14,494 feet the highest point in the contiguous United States, lords over the masses. But such masses! There are over 500 peaks in the Sierra Nevada over 12,000 feet in elevation. The Kern River trail had been my stairway to the gods.

At our junction with the Muir Trail, we were met by a Trailer foursome coming from Mt. Whitney, a few miles to the southeast. Their confident tale of a climb of Whitney the previous day — the first ascent in nearly a month due to the May storms — decided us to backtrack through an afternoon snow flurry and have a go at the peak. I am an armchair mountaineer by nature: if the mountain is agreeable, I am willing to meet it halfway; if it is going to put up an argument, it can go stew in its own snow. The next day found Mt. Whitney in a pleasantly hospitable mood.

We climb, sometimes following the switchback trail, other times heading up the fall-line through the one- to two-foot snowpack. At the summit ridge, we are rewarded with sun to warm numbed feet, and water to ease parched throats. The desiccating quality of the air above 13,000 feet is overwhelming, leaving one with a case of perpetual morning-mouth. Our break is enlivened by stunning views of Mt. Irvine, looming tall and bulky across a 2000-foot chasm with a backdrop of thunderheads. Moving ponderously and keeping a watchful eye on the clouds building up in the east, we push on toward the summit.

The view from the top of Mt. Whitney is what dreams are made of. Certainly what posters are made of. Intricately patterned worlds of rock and snow confront the eye at every turn, as if I were sitting inside a mountain kaleidoscope. Along the precipitous north and east faces, mists rise from the netherworld to pay homage to the Mountain King. My head spins freely in the rarified air, sharpening my focus and cutting my appetite.

Faced by such a presence, I am merely tourist and soon turn to leave. Sailing this alpine sea, I race the snowy spindrift down-mountain, then break camp in the expected afternoon storm. I float the evening on a raft of total exhaustion, just reward for a day at the top of my world. And how rare a day that the mountain should be so inviting and host only one party of four.

The morning is crackly clear, the peaks a study in bas-relief, seeming close enough to touch. The pack, hovering around sixty pounds now, becomes a part of my body like a coat of feathers. Feeling prime, hiking easily through open forests of foxtail pine to retrace my steps to Wallace Creek. Then to resume the chase of

*Polaris . . . I'll put the crafty bugger behind me
yet.*

Met a hiker today whose pack is now down
*to one hundred pounds. He's carrying forty-five
pounds in camera equipment alone. A five-
person tent; food for his Samoyed. And he
hikes in sneakers, with sandals as back-up
footwear. Rather than cross Forester Pass tomorrow, he's going to sit a spell at some alpine
lake, waiting for the ice to break for some fishing. I purely can't believe I have found a Trailer
more off-the-wall than the fellows with the
lawnchairs strapped to their packs.*

*It is too cold to move. Filling the morning
water bottle in Tyndall Creek, the water droplets on the bottle's lip freeze before I even bring
the lid up to cap it. The sun's first rays can be
warming at 11,000 feet, but the plateau below
Forester Pass plays host to a fierce wind. Stag-
gering gusts rifle across the flatlands. As the
walls of Cal Tech Peak and Diamond Mesa
funnel me towards the pass, the richocheting
wind plays me like a pinball wizard. We thread
our way up the avalanche-chute trail to Forester Pass, high point of the Pacific Crest trail
at 13,180 feet. Then bounding, glissading, we
swoop down the sun-softened slope, whooping
and hollering like schoolboys playing hooky at
a creekside ropeswing.*

The Sierra Nevada is a unique range, consisting of a single granite fault block nearly 400 miles
long and 60 to 80 miles wide. It has been folded and
fractured within an inch of its life, suffered the
ravages of local glaciation, and succumbed to the
ever-present erosional agents of temperature and
precipitation. The result is a land of serrated peaks

and ridges, and long, flowing, U-shaped canyons containing strings of lakes and tarns below high alpine meadows.

The trail through the High Sierra follows a repetitive pattern of first climbing an 11,000-12,000 foot pass, then descending into a basin of lakes at the head of a glaciated stream canyon, then dropping off sharply to the 8500-9500 foot level to cross a major stream, from which it begins a climb to another pass. In the ten days of hiking from Mt. Whitney to the town of Mammoth Lakes, my trail crossed eight passes, ranging from 13,180-foot Forester Pass in the south to 10,800-foot Duck Pass in the north.

The nature of the trail and snow conditions dictated a particular hiking strategy. Each night's camp was situated so that our early morning climb to the 11,000-foot south slope snowline would put us there before the snowpack became softened by the sun. If our timing was up to crack, we would have firm footing nearly all the way up to the pass, yet a cushiony surface for the initial, glissading descent. After slogging down to beneath the 10,000-foot snowline of the north slope, we spent lazy afternoons, airing wet boots and bodies in the late spring sun, and reading Farquhar's *History of the Sierra Nevada,* being humbled and exhilarated by the exploits of the immigrants and of Clarence King and John Muir. As evening approached, we would gather up our packs and wade down the snowmelt-flooded trail to camp.

After Forester Pass, the foursome split up. It had been a pleasantly lax association, rarely hiking as a group, sometimes not even camping as one. A comfortable pattern, providing for both isolation and companionship as the spirit so moved. Yet it *was* a group, burdened by a group's tempering of the individual and a cumbersome decision-making process. At Wallace Creek, our discussion on whether to backtrack for an attempt on Whitney had been almost comical in its indecisiveness until the other Trailer foursome arrived to serve as a catalyst for the decision. After the split, Rick and I continued on as a pair for awhile. We were ideally matched, preferring to hike alone, not talking unless there was something to be said. When a dwindling food supply necessitated my moving on ahead, it was with some ambivalence that I made the break.

A couple of bears come snuffling about our camp during the night. Bears are great believers in the conservation of energy: at Vidette Meadows, two miles below us and a major access point to the High Sierra, the pickins are easy. The lodgepole pines about our camp had been too frail to support bear-bagging our food. In our packs by our heads, the aroma of "a little something" brought them a'calling. We were not gracious hosts, banging on pots and cups, hollering and whistling and flashing our Mallorys. Surprisingly, they took the hint.

The Sierra Nevada is famed for the oppressive inquisitiveness and garbage-dump appetites of its bears. During a summer I spent in Yosemite's Tuolumne Meadows several years ago, marauding bears ate three potscrubbers and my Guinness Book of World Records, not to mention the more palatable comestibles within reach. They even made an attempt on a can of motorcycle oil and several attempts on our food-laden VW Bug. Despite any number of bear-bagging strategies designed to put one's food beyond Brother Bruin's salivating grasp, it is a time-honored saying that "a good bear will always beat a good backpacker." I was greatly surprised, then, to not see, hear or play unwilling innkeeper to any bears in the Sierra after the one night above Vidette Meadows.

We had camped over seven miles short of Pinchot Pass and set out expecting sun-softened snow. But expectations are only set in the mind; I know of no way to forewarn the body of the grueling ordeal of tightwiring across snowfields that make random grabs for the crotch, the metamorphosed crust taking trophy scalps from calves and knees at each inadvertent plunge. I move up onto a shattered rock ridge as I approach the pass, my body long since set on automatic pilot. Instinct guides my feet and hands to proper holds; I am mere observer.

But the reward, my God, the treasures at the end of this ragged rainbow of a pass ... the grand arc of ice-sculpted summits across the way, highlights set off by snow and sky ... the delicate pearls of iced tarns in the basin below ... and mare's-tail clouds feathering over the whole. Sitting down below now, sunning on a lakeside granite slab, it's as if it had never happened. The body forgets so easily its discomforts, only remembering the pleasures of the eyes.

A blind Trailer walked into my camp last night. Not functionally blind, of course, but effectively so. He had come 23 miles that day. This morning I leave camp as he awakens. Although it is less than two miles to Selden Pass, he catches me up shortly before reaching the top and is already heading down the other

*side when I get there. A bit of a shame, really.
The sun has just topped the ridge guarding the
east edge of Marie Lake and, through wisps of
cirrus cloud, is casting a soft glow over the
contours of the Mono Divide and sequining the
snow at my feet.*

*My aesthetic sense is slowly being over-
whelmed. Glorious scene after wondrous view
floods my eyes like so much snowmelt. It is a
vast museum into which all my most favored
art has been placed. I wonder how fine is the
line between esctasy and insanity.*

Despite the exceptional grandeur of the High
Sierra, I would not remember my time there as the
most enjoyable experience of the trek, not even the
most pleasurable in California. This was due in
part to the season. The magically pellucid,
aquamarine waters of its lakes were largely ice-
bound, colorless. The rugged delicacy of its alpine
fell-fields was buried under a uniform mat of
white. The many-splendored wildflower world of
its meadows was yet a brownish bog of yesteryear's
life.

Even more responsible perhaps were the con-
straints on the marathon walker and the eyes I
used to see with. There was an insidious, subsurface pressure to keep moving, to put some slight
fraction of the path behind me each day, which only
rarely subsided. As mile after mile, day after day,
of the High Sierra's exalted mountainscape passed
before my eyes in review, it began to take on a
wearying sameness. Particularly when viewed
through the macro-eyes of the mileage-maker.
Even during the long midday breaks, the macro-
focus I so typically used would often see no more
than Peak, Canyon, Lake. I most often wore the

personna of the Tourist, and the tourist is inherently incapable of "seeing." To the tourist everything is a picture: two-dimensional, lifeless. Of greatest import is gross variety, a steadily changing flow of images.

What was usually missing from my High Sierran experience was the micro-focus of the Resident. Eyes that would see the interrelationships of peak and canyon and lake, the infinite variety in the chipped contours of a ridge. It is only the resident who gains the awareness that comes from watching the evolution over the years of a lake becoming a bog, becoming a meadow, becoming a forest. Such vision and understanding is a function of knowledge and time, each of which I possessed in such relatively small quantities. Enough only to catch a faint glimmering of the living world around me . . . and to know how much I was missing.

The journey would continue as a never-ending series of trade-offs between the dichotomous worlds of Tourist and Resident. The Sierra only seemed to represent the conflict with greater clarity. As a hummingbird flitting back and forth between the two perspectives, I learned to take my pleasure from the experience as a whole, rather than from predetermined qualities. Fortunately, I came to an understanding of the singular nature of this marathon trek early on. Only three weeks from Mexico, the journal had mused:

> I view this journey as similar to the captain's platter at a seafood restaurant. I am being served a little bit of everything with no choice as to preparation. When I've finished, though, I will know which items I want to order again and how I wish them seasoned: early summer for wildflowers on this one, late summer for ice-free climbing on that.

Ahhhright! After some 150 miles of high-country walking, I've come upon, right here at Purple Lake, my first real, live, honest-to-goodness "deep greens and blues are the colors I choose," Sierran alpine lake – with great hunks of beautiful rock 'round it. Oh, all the dozens of previous lakes qualify for the title, of course, but they lose a world of style points, what with being iced over and all.

And let me just say this about these mountains here. The Sierra Nevada is so rich in gorgeous rock that you could take any one of these summits the folks around here haven't deigned to even measure for a number, much less name. You could take it and stick it back in the Appalachians, and they'd not only give it a title, they'd name a state after it . . . or at least a horse race, or a bluegrass festival.

My food supply gave out before the John Muir Trail did, and I took a short sidetrip into a ski-resort town of Mammoth Lakes to resupply. A pleasing hamlet if it weren't for the disturbing death rattle to be heard at every turn, due to the low snow year in the Sierra and its disastrous effect on the local ski industry. I was taken in, washed and polished, and stuffed to the gills with food and civilized decadence. My cookstove, which shortly out of Weldon had become first reluctant, then adamantly opposed to giving flame, had its clogged part replaced in a local backpacking shop. Added to my belongings was a natural history book for the Sierra Nevada, an earnest effort to bridge the gap between Tourist and Resident.

My body was catered to further on my first night out of Mammoth as camp was made at the hot springs of Reds Meadow. Nearby was the striking display of Devils Postpile National Monument. A rack of tightly-jointed, five- and six-sided columns, each a hundred feet high and little more than a foot in diameter, it was formed when andesitic lava flows cooled to their characteristic polygonal structure. It is showing its age: glaciers have planed the tops of the columns to a uniform height and polished their surface; thousands of years of weathering have loosened the bonds that hold the columns together, and now a pile of crumbled "posts" lies at the foot of the formation.

Beyond the Devils Postpile, I began to wind through two days of stunning alpine lake country in the Ritter Range, before making my way up to a final high pass. At 11,056 feet, Donohue Pass marked my departure from the real High Sierra and my entry into Yosemite National Park.

Since Mt. Whitney, the perfection of the weather has been matched only by the perfection of the High Sierra mountainscape. However, a new weather pattern has set in during the past few days. Hazy, mostly sunny mornings give way to cloud as midday approaches. Rumbles of thunder usher an obscured sun past its zenith. The wind finds its voice and joins in accompaniment. Then the early afternoon rain, sans wind. A gentle, enduring rain, an Oregon rain. And I experience again how soothing and peaceful it is to walk alone in a quiet rain. How the mists encircle me and hold me warmly, intimately, to the bosom of the forest. The world lightens as the clouds lift and splotch with early evening blue. The night will play a duet of sprinkles and stars before yielding again to the morning sun.

The mosquitos advance their front lines to well over 10,000 feet during the night. Brief but violent skirmishes are fought throughout the early part of the morning, with losses moderate on both sides. The mosquitos are fighting a brilliant strategic battle, positioning their strongest forces near every source of water. My plan is to carry out a delaying action through the day, establishing myself in the defensive stronghold of 11,000-foot Donohue Pass for the night. Then set up a perimeter defense with the thiamine tablets for the descent into Tuolumne Meadows tomorrow.

Meanwhile, the home front is racked with internal dissension. The Stomach is staging continual demonstrations in protest of government policies and has enlisted the aid of the renowned terrorist group, the Bowels, whose presence is already being felt. Members of the group took over an important government outpost during the night and are already making several inconveniencing runs from their new command post. Although the affairs of state continue uninterrupted, there is the danger of significant disruption if a settlement is not reached soon. One hopes that the national holiday, to be proclaimed upon arrival in Tuolumne Meadows, will bring a calm to these troubled waters.

In matters pitting the heart against the mind, reason has always had the final say ... until last night. My heart was set on sleeping atop Donohue Pass, my rite of passage into Yosemite. The afternoon rains having abated according to schedule, I set off for the pass and my last night above 10,000 feet. My mind was a bit concerned with the bank of pillowy grey looming in the western sky, but my heart would

*have none of it. For four days now the afternoon
rains had yielded to glowing evenings and
spacious nights. Shunning my tent, I spread
out a simple groundcloth and bedded down to
greet the stars.*

*The stars fell in liquid drops, then in a
colder crystalline form. Wrapped in my poncho, I managed to keep my lower body dry
while my down bag collapsed coldly about my
shoulders. Morning's first light found me quite
thoroughly awake, thirteen miles from security. Dressed in nearly every piece of clothing I
had, I stumbled through the now trail-less
snow, falling ever thicker in great, wet, blind-
ing clots. A momentary hiatus about midway
to have hot chocolate with some more mindful
hikers. Then continuing, boots leadened by the
slush and fordless steams, clothing a cold,
clammy straitjacket. Tuolumne Meadows was
reached in a cold rain, with a hot bath lying
just below the horizon.*

After hitching down the Sierran west slope to
the shelter of Yosemite Valley, I spent two days in
a tent cabin, recovering from the Wet Rat Syndrome I had contracted on my descent from Donohue
Pass. As a raw, natural phenomenon, Yosemite
Valley is without peer; it must have had its own
personal god during the Creation. With late spring
snowmelt at its peak, the Valley's waterfalls filled
the air with their lusty roar, echoing off the glacial
statuary of the soaring, granitic walls. On the valley floor, where mere mortals tread, it was a thriv-
ing, somewhat repugnant, tourist community, a
cross between the Tower of Babel and the
Boardwalk. With fresh supplies gathered and my
physical needs met, I followed my thumb back up
the road to Tuolumne Meadows, to regain the Path.

High Sierra Trail Log

Date	Camp	Elevation	Mileage
May 15	Bull Run Creek	2800	17
16	Ant Canyon	3360	9
17	Brush Creek	4290	10
18	Forks of the Kern	4720	12
19	Kern Flat area	5040	6
20	Grasshopper Flat	5880	11
21	Soda Springs area	6310	6
22	Kern Hot Springs	6880	11
23	Wallace Creek/Muir Trail junction	10,390	12
24	Guitar Lake area	11,590	7
25	Crabtree Ranger Station — Mt. Whitney climb	10,640	3
26	Tyndall Creek	10,960	10
27	Bubbs Creek	10,000*	10
28	Woods Creek	8490	16
29	South Fork Kings River	10,050	11
30	Palisades Creek	9540	10
31	Muir Pass area	10,400	13
June 1	McClure Meadow	9650	12
2	Sally Keyes Lakes	10,160	15
3	Silver Pass area	9600	20
4	Duck Pass	10,880	16
5	Old Mammoth — unplanned supply stop	8000*	4*
6	Reds Meadow Hot Springs	7620	6*
7	Shadow Lake	8750	10
8	Donohue Pass	11060	12
9-10	Yosemite Valley — supply pick-up/ layover day	4000	14
11	Tuolumne Meadows — layover day	8590	—

Totals

283 miles
26 hiking days
2 layover days

*elevation approximate to the nearest 100 feet, mileage approximate to the nearest mile

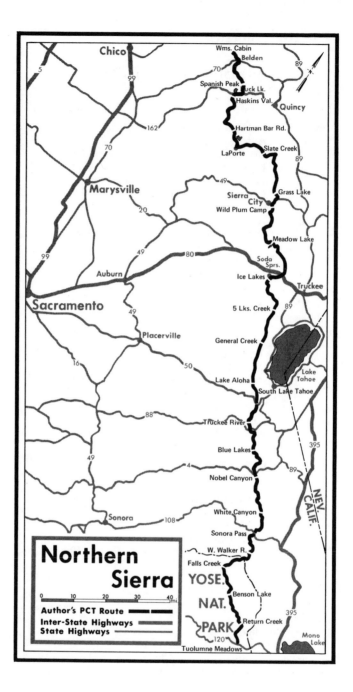

Chico

5

99

70

Wms. Cabin
Belden
89

Spanish Peak
uck Lk.
Haskins Val.
Quincy

162

70

Hartman Bar Rd.

LaPorte
Slate Creek
89

Marysville

20

49

Sierra
City
Wild Plum Camp

Grass Lake

Meadow Lake

99

49

80

Soda
Sprs.

Auburn

Ice Lakes

Truckee
89

Sacramento

49

5 Lks. Creek

Placerville

General Creek

Lake
Tahoe

16

50

Lake Aloha

South Lake Tahoe

88

Truckee River

Blue Lakes

395

49

4

Nobel Canyon

89

Sonora

108

White Canyon

Sonora Pass

W. Walker R.

**Northern
Sierra**

YOSE.

Falls Creek

0   10   20   30   40
mi.

Author's PCT Route
Inter-State Highways
State Highways

NAT.

PARK

Benson Lake

Return Creek

120

Tuolumne Meadows

395

Mono
Lake

NEV.
CALIF.

The Northern Sierra

Tuolumne Meadows is a grand, rambling arena, one of the largest subalpine meadows in the Sierra Nevada. Bisected by the meandering Tuolumne River, it is ringed with peaks and domes of a beautiful, light granitic rock whose surface varies from glacier-polished slick to that of a geologic pincushion, pimpled with nubbins of feldspar. Returning to Tuolumne Meadows was like greeting an old friend. After a narrow escape from the University of Michigan in 1971, I had spent two months playing in the meadows and its environs. The memories came drifting back like a lazy meadow walk: eating soft ice cream cones out front of the canvas monstrosity of the store while reading Art Hoppe and Doonesbury in day-old Chronicles . . . the climbers congregating around the storeside picnic tables, to talk in their strange tongue — five-eight, five-ten, all-free, bombproof-hold . . . the soda spring, still enclosed by its ramshackle log hutch . . . the nightly visitations of Brother Bruin.

North of Tuolumne Meadows, the Pacific Crest Trail follows the beginnings of the Tahoe-Yosemite trail. The relatively gentle terrain between Mammoth and the Meadows was a thing of the past as the path headed into the "washboard topography" of the northern Yosemite backcountry. Like a great, granite army closing ranks, the ridges piled up against each other, separated by the glacial troughs of Virginia Canyon, Matterhorn Canyon, Stubblefield Canyon, Jack Main Canyon, etc. Shunning the path of least resistance, the trail insisted on pushing perpendicular to the grain of the country, commonly squeezing several thousand-foot-plus ridge climbs and bone-jarring descents into a dayful of miles.

Former Trailer companions were also left behind, but new Trailers appeared to fill the gap: Don and Monte, who had tossed in with each other after their initial partners had left the trail and whose lockstep hiking style reinforced my reluctance to travel in a group; and Joe, a fellow-Oregonian with whom I also had in common the pre-journey baking of dozens, even hundreds, of pounds of granola. Although rarely hiking in a party, I often found my evenings spent in company with one or more of these folks, especially after my supposedly clean-burning, LP cartridge cookstove clogged on me again two days out of Tuolumne.

I've caught a touch of the blue funk. One aspect of the malady is a perverse twist to the old saying, "The way to a man's heart is through his stomach." The stomach's tactic this morning is to make me feel total revulsion at the mere thought of food. It is mid-morning before I can slip a little something past the ringleader of the palace revolt in my intestines.

Of far greater influence on my general feeling of malaise is a sense of journey's end. Throughout the planning of this venture, the High Sierra had been wrapped in a mystique of physical peril and imminent insanity, the image of four weeks of snowshoeing in solitude lurking in the dark corners of my mind. Past Tuolumne Meadows, I had figured, the journey would be summer warmth and earthen trails and vacationing companions, all downhill for the remaining four months. I carried this mind-set next to my heart right on through the relatively painless three weeks on the Muir

Trail, setting myself up for the anticlimactic feeling I'm now experiencing.

The Ambivalence Blues, Opus 71
I got the Am-bivalence Blues,
The Am-bivalence Blues, it's said.
I got the Am-bivalence Blues,
It's the Am-bivalence Blues I dread.
Well, my feets got theys travelin' shoes on . . .
But my heart feels like it's filled with lead.

A memory of adventure past: grinding up the 1500 vertical feet from Benson Lake to Seavey Pass in the northern Yosemite backcountry. Swimming through a sea of mosquitos and cursing the very notion of backpacking. Then passing through a narrow gap and coming to . . . The Tarn. The quintessential Sierran tarn: ringed with great slabs of glacier-polished granite for sunning, with water so clear that I was knee-deep before I realized I'd broken the surface. My, my, but it had made it all worthwhile.

Today, the Tarn welcomes me back, its message fades not one whit in the six years I've been gone.

On summer afternoons, when it is just a shade too warmish for the mosquitos to be out exercising, it is still possible to make a climb out of a canyon much more pleasant than it has any right to be. You can, for instance, find yourself two or three deer who don't mind terribly if you tag along fifty feet behind their leisurely browse. Or you can whip out your natural history book every now and again and identify a few wildflowers: mule ears, pussypaws, forget-me-nots, phlox, western wallflower. Or decipher the gnarled convolu-

*tions of the trunk of a rockbound whitebark
pine. But then I crest the ridge, where it's
cooler, and start down its shady north side,
where it's moister. The mosquitos are up from
their midday siesta, looking for a little something to have at teatime. My pleasures are back
riding the rays of the sun.*

Mosquitos. They did not appear until I was
nearing Yosemite and, once I was north of Lake
Tahoe, they were rarely more than an evening
nuisance except in southern Oregon (thanks and a
tip of the hiking staff to the drought for minimizing
their impact). During their heyday, however, they
were a plague to make the God of the Israelites
proud. Hikers crossing a soggy Sierran meadow
appeared to be celebrants at a festival of St. Vitus.

In an odd example of the old bromide, "Its bark
is worse than its bite," the presence of mosquitos
was for me a greater annoyance than their actual
nipping. Squadrons of the little buggers tickling
my legs and enveloping my head with their mad-
dening hum would send me windmilling down the
trail in an exercise of consciousless movement.
Rest breaks were stand-up, perpetual motion affairs; hardly restful. Evening camps were planned
so that the most heavily infested meadows would
be crossed in the early morning, the night's freez-
ing temperatures keeping the skeeters in bed till
mid-morning.

However, with my mosquito-netted tent in the
evenings, and long clothing — my thin, red, nylon
windbreaker was a remarkable repellent; I un-
explicably suffered only perhaps a half-dozen bites
through it during the entire journey — and a
reasonably effective chemical repellent, I was able
to escape relatively unpunctured. The wind, too,

was a comrade in arms, upsetting their flight patterns, making them career helplessly off the runway. And unlike those angry welts that I remember once keeping me in a frenzy until the next day's mosquitos had a chance to afflict new punishment, the bites this summer seemed almost to disappear before I had a chance to scratch.

Vignettes ... Walker Meadows, dew-sequined in the slant of the early morning sun, mists simmering above a small tarn, Sierra shooting stars a purple-glisten on the green ... looking south from the saddle above Kennedy Canyon to the grand maze of northern Yosemite, waves of snow-creased ridges like whitecaps at the beach ... Leavitt Lake, a limpid pearl of moisture beneath the stark, volcanic hills of the northern Sierra.

At Dorothy Lake Pass the trail passed out of Yosemite National Park. The park boundary is a creation of man, of course, but this is one time that man has followed nature's course. South of the boundary are the rhythmic ridges and canyons of Yosemite's largely igneous rock. North of the boundary, the northern Sierra begins to show the influence of the volcanics of the southern Cascades. Rock of chocolate browns, reds, greens and purples replaced the light grey shadings of the previous month. The trail had moved from granitic bedrock to volcanic rubble.

Having left the familiar High Sierran geology behind me, I grew excited again, eager to see what was around the next bend, over the next ridge. This was not as easily accomplished as it had been in the High Sierra. Although the elevation of timberline was descending as I moved north, the topographic elevations were declining even more rapidly due to

the northwestward decline of the Sierran range.
The highest passes were now struggling to reach
9000 feet, rarely getting their heads above timberline. Now off the northern Yosemite washboard,
the trail took on a more even disposition. Its rolling
treadmill dropped down into the art museum of
White Canyon, where groves of aspen and
lodgepole pine, with primitive symbols and figures
carved into their trunks, demonstrated the creativ-
ity of the Basque sheepherder's knife. The Path
crossed several of the principal trans-Sierra im-
migrant routes of the mid-19th century — Sonora
Pass, Ebbetts Pass, Carson Pass — as it carried me
north toward Lake Tahoe.

> *Met two new Trailers the other day at*
> *Leavitt Meadows Resort. Mark and Marty, the*
> *San Diego Truckers, who started the trail two*
> *weeks before I did. Their experience has been a*
> *tad adventuresome: finding a dead body in the*
> *rest room of a deserted service station, sitting*
> *under three feet of fresh-fallen snow in their*
> *Whitney area camp, suffering frostbitten feet in*
> *their crossing of Forester Pass in whiteout*
> *conditions with sixty mile-an-hour winds. By*
> *comparison, my journey has been positively –*
> *ahem – pedestrian.*

The San Diego Truckers . . . the Trailer name-
game started up in the front ranks, among those
folks who began the trail in late March. I first
began hearing the names at the Gathering in Weldon, where retreating Trailers had returned with
stories from the front. But it was not until Trailers
reached the trail registers in the Sierra that the
names seemed to come into common usage. Inter-
mingled with the everyday names of weekenders
on short loop trips were the monikers of the

Mexico-to-Canada Trailers: The Bay Area Bombers, Strider, the Kelty Kids, the Chairman, the Seattle Spikers, the Portland Trailblazers.

As the months passed, the number of Trailers still on the quest dwindled; there was even some attrition among those in the vanguard. Yet the names kept marching on. The effect was comical at times: I met two young fellows hiking south on the Oregon section of the trail. They had passed several groups of Trailers during their past week on the trail and they didn't at first believe that my name was only David.

What a glorious morning. I leave early, before the others have breakfasted, to climb to the plateau above the valley of the Upper Truckee River. Long streaks of cloud glisten brilliantly above the hills across the way. To the northeast, down the dusty green avenue of the valley's forested floor, lies the hazy silver-blue of Lake Tahoe. It is this morning that inspires the trek. It is this morning I walk forever.

The trail approaches Lake Tahoe but remains aloof, never mingling with the burgeoning development along its shores. Besides, there is company enough as one enters the Desolation Wilderness west of the lake. Perhaps it's the multitude of glacier-crafted alpine lakes, flush with trout; perhaps it's the proximity to the casinos on Lake Tahoe's south shore. Whatever the attraction, Desolation Wilderness is one of the most popular wilderness areas in California — boulder-to-boulder backpackers.

It was only a couple of days, however, before the trail moved me on to a more gentle country and still lower elevations. Wilderness walkers remained behind. In fact, all walkers remained be-

hind: but for a brief encounter with Don and
Monte, dinnering at a lakeside resort one week out
of Tahoe, I would not see another Trailer until
reaching the slopes of Mt. Hood in northern Oregon, two months hence. Sometimes a week or more
would pass between sightings of a backpacker of
any stripe. The path, richly forested, had entered
the realm of the logger. Logging trucks were now
my occasional companions, hauling the selective
mowings of Jeffrey, sugar and yellow pine, white
fir, cedar. Sharing the same habitat as the loggers
were the dirt bikes, the RV's. I had come out of the
wilderness, into the Machine Age of Recreation. It
was rarely pleasant company.

I had also entered gold country. The Tahoe National Forest map is littered with indications of
placer diggings. Some mines are still active, and it
was not surprising to see a person ambling along a
backroad, fishing pole in one hand, mining pan in
the other.

Summer had arrived in the mountains. It was
not only written on the calendar, but also on the
waters, warmer now to the touch and the tongue,
and on the trail, where sneaker prints now out-
numbered those of lug soles. The pack was slimmed
down, now carrying only my summer wardrobe.
Wool underclothes and down overclothes were sent
home, and the heavyweight boots I had been wearing since Weldon were exchanged for my lightweight trail shoes. My body had long ago completed its essential summer trim, yet it continued
to hone down its edges. Letters to friends described
me as having bodybuilder legs on the torso of a
prisoner-of-war.

It is like southern California again: new
logging roads rampant on the green field of

outdated maps. The path is eventually found, as are a few moments' rest above Bear Lake. Anxiety melts in the stillness, as the breathing of the red-fir forest plays rhythm line to birdsong.

I will camp tonight below 6500 feet, the lowest evening elevation since the Kern River canyon over a month ago. I've come to the lowlands of the north Sierra with its year-round population. My walk is undergoing a transformation. From pure wilderness experience of varying isolation, I return to a journey through rural America. I appreciate the change, in a way. I now use civilization in the way that, as a cityfolk, I ordinarily had used the wilderness: as a brief hiatus to refresh myself for day-to-day life. And to pull the taste buds out of cold storage.

With the lowering of elevation has come a sharp change in my surroundings. Still gently rolling ridges and valleys on the face of it, of course, but I've dropped out of the open forests of lodgepole pine and red fir. Now I have back my old friend Jeffrey "Butterscotch" Pine, the rich greens and shaggy body of incense cedar, and Christmas tree stands of white fir. Thickly forested, the valley floors are lush with ferns and grasses, cradling me deep in Mother E's arms.

North Fork American River ... ask someone where they'd like to be on a hot summer's afternoon and they might say something like, oh, small mountain stream, with trilling cascades and eddying pools, and great rock slabs all about for sunning. Maybe have the path to it wind through a valley wildflower garden:

paintbrush, lupine, mule ears, western wallflower, forget-me-not, pussypaws, larkspur, snowplant, phlox, western mountain aster. Set it all in a park of aspen, with a few firs and pines scattered about for texture. Then bring in a bit of a breeze, just to temper the heat and set the aspen to twinkling in the sun. That should about do it, ah-yup.

Nearly all dirt road today. Roads are rhythm-makers, pickin' 'em up and layin' 'em down. But my ankles discover that I have the lower-cut boots back and have begun to take liberties, twisting themselves three ways from Sunday. If roads are rhythm-makers, wrenched ankles are rhythm-benders. I cruise down this road in syncopated time.

It is amazing how little it takes to become injured when under a pack, and how accustomed one becomes to living with such disablements. I saw Trailers walking on feet so badly blistered and awkwardly bandaged that they looked like victims of war atrocities. Seemingly inverse arches, descent-swollen knees, hips inflamed to a baboon-butt-red by a chafing hipbelt, lower-back spasms brought on from staying too long in the harness. Early in the trek — Big Bear City, Weldon — the Trailer gatherings looked like gimpyleg conventions.

Though I brushed up against most of the common maladies from time to time, my personal affliction was my ankles. Disturbingly tractable joints, they received their most extreme distortion on the rocky backroads of the northern Sierra . . . a tiny moment of imbalance and, all of a sudden, tendons and ligaments that weren't used to doing diddlysquat found themselves sole support of 200 teetering pounds. My gait, so natural and rhythmic only moments before, would become a movement of unparalleled grotesquery. There was nothing for it but to continue down the road, eventually evening out to a doddering pace as the offended joint was massaged by the continued motion.

Yet, regardless of how violently I had wrenched the ankle the previous day, I always awoke with no perceptible swelling. There would be just a tenderness and stiffness that usually worked itself out in the first hour of walking. My recuperative ability never failed to amaze me. It fair boggled the mind, which was probably why my mind let the body take care of itself.

Sugar pine! There I am, just idling through a cozy back corner of my forest, making no stir but for scaring up an occasional deer, and there they are: two gargantuan cones. Sugar pine; there's no mistaking the cones, but I have yet to meet the tree. I pull out the natural history book and look about for their owner. There it be ... cinnamon-scaly trunk that goes up forever before meeting with tremendous limbs sticking straight out from its sides ... the forest's scarecrow. What an odd, fascinating creature. So pleased to make your acquaintance.

It has been a long day. From first light to last, 27 miles – quite the longest day thus far. My surroundings were a bit blurred, but it was a pleasant sensation, like undulating gently on a warm waterbed. And, oh, those moments of clarity! The sun's first rays working their coloring craft on the crags of Sierra Buttes ... Deer Lake, lying cooly placid beneath a stand

*of red fir ... the endless billows of forested
hills, pocked with woodland lakes, creased by
infant streams ... the cooling, quiet welcome of
thick stands of middle-growth white fir, whose
bees were befuddled by the red-windbreakered
flower that yielded no pollen ... the deer on
McRae Ridge, caught in mid-stride as it came
upon me at rest, body straining forward as
mind flew in retreat, finally breaking its
momentary paralysis to pogo up the ridge ...
the old man camped at McRae Meadows, from
Wales by way of Vermont and the northern
California coast: "I've been coming to these
meadows for twenty years. I'm 73 now. One of
the last men who knows how to make slate
roofing by hand."*

The Big Push. I built my rationale with care,
like a house of cards. The overwhelming spectacle
of the High Sierra was past; except for the
glaciated volcanic crags of Sierra Buttes and the
3000-foot chasms of the Feather River's Middle
and North forks, the Sierra here wore its least
dramatic raiments. And with much of the permanent Crest Trail still on the drawing boards, the
designated route was primarily an unattractive
blend of logging roads and county highways, crea-
tured with noxious machines. I wished to put it
behind me quickly, and save my leisure for the
mellow grandeur of the Oregon Cascades. Besides,
there were homefolks who might wish to join me
for a few days slowboatin' through those mountains,
and with whom I might want to rest a spell. Yet the
slow days in the High Sierra had dropped me behind my paper schedule and I did not relish the
thought of pushing the trek into the early snows of
a Washington October. I needed time, more time.

As I could not add days to the calendar, I set about adding hours to my days. It was early summer. Waking to the dawn roar of logging trucks, playing outside till the streetlights came on, my hourglass was bloated with the sands of daylight. I had learned early on that miles passed more readily with increased time on the trail, rather than by stepping my pace up a notch or two. So I gathered up a couple weeks of summer's endless days and began feeding them through my mileage meter. In the 14 days of the Big Push, I would cover 296 miles.

It's a sultry, overcast day. Still, sticky air. Folks sitting out front of the LaPorte store, waiting for the mail and talking rain. Some even go so far as predicting it, but there haven't been but five or six drops all morning. And two of them landed on me ... with little effect: I'm still filthy. The forests remain just so much giant tinder. The fire danger, extreme to begin with, doesn't even register on the scale with the fourth of July camper-circus about to commence.

Talking trout. Best trout-fishing in California can be found on the Middle Fork of the Feather River just up the road, they tell me. Caught twenty trout in fifteen minutes one time, all better than eighteen inches, they tell me. I don't fish, I say, have no pole. Ought to add a touch of skepticism, just to keep the stories rolling, but I am a stranger in town.

Pitching the tent on a patch of roadside gravel as a young fellow drives by on my dirt road. He stops, asks if I am doing the Crest Trail. He had started the trail three years before only to have his journey aborted after four days by a severe leg infection. He had sat at trailside and cried. Now he has a family, a job, all the trappings and traps of life in the mainstream, and I am a spur for feelings of envy and regret. We talk for half an hour or more; he never leaves his car. Nearly dark then, he drives away.

It had cleared in the evening. Enough so that I spread out sleeping bag on poncho as I prepared to bed. But the few clouds in the west had the feeling of Donohue Pass. Tent up, I fall asleep in a gentle rain . . . the kind of rain that is a sensual pleasure to wake up to, a rain to feed dreams.

The morning is walked in some sun, some clouds and some consternation. Four miles into the day and I am sent off on a detour. It is a bit galling to be put on a temporary detour from the temporary trail, but the loggers must have their ridge. There was nothing for it but to blindly trust the Forest Service signs to lead me back to the Path, akin to playing Russian roulette with a gun someone else has loaded. Fortune is with me; I come up with an empty chamber.

An afternoon storm, painting the Feather's Middle Fork in dull greens and grays, hits just as I arrive. It clears long enough for a quick dip in the welcoming pool at Hartman Bar. Then the rain returns. I cut my hiking teeth in the southern Appalachians and grew to love forest rain-walking. There is a magical intimacy to walking cloaked only in mist, accompanied only by ferns and sheltering timber.

It is like coming home. The richly forested hills rolling off into the distance, tying down

*the horizon, look so much like the Cascades.
But then, they are the Cascades. At my feet lies
the 3000-foot chasm of the Feather River's
North Fork. In those hills beyond, with a few
last granitic gasps, the Sierra Nevada will
meet its end. I have been playing nearly nine
weeks in this Range of Light. Now I am to enter
the Land of Vulcan. It feels good to be home.*

Northern Sierra Trail Log

Date	Camp	Elevation	Mileage
June 12	Return Creek/McCabe Creek confluence	8540	14
13	Benson Lake	7550	17
14	Falls Creek	7970	16
15	West Fork West Walker River	8610	16
16	Sonora Pass	9630	15
17	White Canyon crest	8840	12
18	Nobel Canyon	8320	16
19	Lower Blue Lake	8060	22
20	Upper Truckee River	8320	14
21	South Lake Tahoe — supply pick-up	6250	11
22	Lake Aloha	8160	10
23	General Creek	7200	16
24	Five Lakes Creek	6350	17
25	Ice Lakes area	6870	20
26	Meadow Lake	7290	20
27	Wild Plum Campground	4480	20
28	Grass Lake area	6350	12
29	Slate Creek	5920	27
30	Hartman Bar Ridge road — supply pick-up in LaPorte	5520	23
July 1	Haskins Valley area	5900*	25*
2	Spanish Peak	7020	12*
3	Rex Williams cabin	3700	21

Totals
376 miles
22 hiking days

*elevation approximate to the nearest 100 feet, mileage
approximate to the nearest mile

Ashland
Bull Gap
Cook & Green Pass
Donomore Mdws.
Happy
Camp
Seiad Valley
66
140
Klamath
Falls
96
5
OREGON
CALIFORNIA
97
Big Ridge
Kidder Creek
3
Yreka
Etna
Mule Bridge
Trail Ck. Camp
Weed
Masterson
Meadow
Coffee Creek
Toad Lake
Upper Castle Crags
Dunsmuir

Northern
California

0   10   20   30 mi.

Author's PCT Route ▬▬▬
Inter-State Highways ▬▬▬
State Highways ▬▬▬

3
5
Castle Crags S.P.
Cabin Creek
89
Deer Creek
Nelson Ck.
Lake
Shasta
Burney Falls S.P.
299
Burney
Redding
5
44
Cave Camp
Old
Station
LASSEN
VOLC.N.P.
89
44
36
Red
Bluff
Warner Val. Camp
5
Gurnsey Ck. Camp
99
36
Humboldt Summit
32
Belden
89
Wms. Cabin
70

Northern California

Long ago, giving welcome to strangers was a way of life. Rex Williams is a moment of long ago. His small hut stands open to the wilderness traveler, regardless of whether he is there to play host. He was at his place when I arrived last night, so I had more than just the sign on the door to extend warm greetings. We talked only sporadically then, but this morning the good hiking hours of early sun are lost to Rex, his company and hotcakes-and-fried-egg breakfast. He is a man to spend rainy days with over a checkerboard in the general store, spittin' on the potbelly stove to punctuate comments on the guv'mint in Washington and what the loggers is doin' to the canyon. Sitting outside on this fine summer's morning, talking mining and younger days, Rex Williams is a diamond in the rough.

*I watch the spectrum of color narrow as the
set follows the sun below the horizon. A feeling
of quiet melancholia filters in, a valley fog beneath my peaks of joy. I wish there were a
friend here to lie beside me and share the
evening; it is so lovely.*

*As night deepens, a valley town glimmers
in the distance. I've a balcony seat for their
Independence Day spectacular and soon tiny
prickles of light arc above the town. Sitting
snugly bagged on my windy knoll, I ooh and
aah at the especially bright ones and occasional multiples. Then collapse, giggling un-
controllably at this bizarre juxtaposition of
wilderness and civilization.*

Although no geologic kin to the northern
Sierra, the southern Cascades mirror its suffering
under the scourge of civilization. Mankind's ebb
and flow — the mines, the logging, the ranches, the
hydroelectric dams and power plants, the recreational development — wash across the land, dilut-
ing its features, eroding away the excitement of
wilderness that once was.

The Land of Vulcan did not wait long to issue its
greeting, however. The Path soon led me into Lassen Volcanic National Park: volcanism with a ven-
geance. Geysers, cinder cones, fumaroles, lava
beds, steaming lakes looking like split-pea soup
with their surface film of high-temperature algae.
Then there is 10,457-foot Lassen Peak itself, whose
1915-1921 eruptions were the most recent of any
volcano in the continental United States. A dacite
plug dome, Lassen does not share the more sym-
metrical, towering beauty of its stratovolcano
cousins to the north. Its broad, lumpy body looms
above the surrounding countryside like an ogre.

North of Lassen, evidence of the new geologic
realm continued, ranging from a roadside, walk-
through lava tube near the head of Hat Creek
Valley to the extraordinary beauty of Burney Falls
at its base. Burney Creek is springfed, tapping a
massive subterranean reservoir. Groundwater has
also filtered through the porous volcanic rock un-
derriding the impervious creekbed to create an
ephemeral bridalveil of smaller falls as a striking
backdrop to the main cascades.

Burney Falls had a significance beyond its
aesthetic appeal. For one thing, it signaled a temporary halt to the trek's northward progress. Still
treading roads for the most part, I began a long,
westward-arcing descent along a chain of reservoirs to the Sacramento River. From Iron Canyon's
bowl of logging-debris soup to the surreal,
aquamarine waters of McCloud, each reservoir
provided the setting for lazy afternoon swim-
siestas. It was warmer now, drier, as summer
heightened and the elevation dwindled. The
character of the forest was transformed from
Mountain Garden to City Park as the thick stands
of fir and pine opened up and were increasingly
infiltrated by deciduous oaks, maples and dog-
wood.

As the change of orientation began at Burney
Falls, the Big Push came to an end. The Push had
been a separate journey. For two weeks, it had
directed my motions like the stars. So much had
been missed; the camera and the natural history
book had rarely left my belly pack. Yet so much
had been gained. I had a much richer, more fully
integrated understanding of how my body follows
the rutted road of my mind's expectations. I had
challenged the limitations set by my past experience and found them to be, like all parameters,

both liberating and stifling. My concept of distance and its relationship to time was amended; a new perspective was added to my mind's portfolio. And the grand journey continued.

Mt. Shasta calls unannounced this morning as I come onto McCloud Reservoir, whose waters are that pellucid turquoise color that is always such a shock to one's sense of perspective. Head down to keep an eye on the road's rocky contours, I stride along its west shore, then look up a moment to find the lake has gained an overseer. Surprisingly barren of snow, Shasta retains its magic nevertheless and adds majesty to my morning.

Tony and his son Bob bring their own magic to my day. There are millions of Bobs and Tonys spinning about the globe yet I seem to meet them only in books. Like modern-day Zorbas, they are excited by the commonplace in life as much as by the fantastical. Yet they've enough sense of self to give as much as they receive. Perhaps more ... after a couple of hours of swimming, fishing and tale-telling in their company, I leave with several zucchinis and potatoes from their garden and a bag of freshly shelled walnuts.

Two peaches, two nectarines, two plums, a small basket of Bing cherries, and damn the consequences. This is my first summer fruit since Tahoe three weeks back. All that the lakeside resorts and gas-station markets have been able to manage have been a few square-bottom-of-the-crate oranges and some mushy, controlled-atmosphere-storage apples. Come on, I would cry, I'm only fifty miles from the Central Valley's fruit kingdom; give me real

*fruit. They would respond with a half-dozen
liver-spotted bananas. I sit out front of the
Dunsmuir market, eating peaches as much for
effect as for sustenance, rivulets of juice
coursing through my beard.*

Under the neighboring eyes of 14,162-foot Mt.
Shasta and the splendid granitic sculpture of Castle Crags, the trail continues its westward heading
as it climbs out of the Sacramento Canyon toward
the Trinity Alps. This great arc to the west, which
it would take over a week of northeastward hiking
to compensate for, seemed at first a rather exag-
gerated detour. It certainly was not designed for
economic reasons: estimates of the cost of chiseling
the final few miles of permanent trail into the
Marble Mountains range as high as $40,000 per
mile. However, despite its steering wide of Mt.
Shasta, the westward swing provides for more consistently mountainous terrain than any of the
more direct northward routes.

Too, in skirting the northern border of the
Salmon-Trinity Alps Wilderness and then bending
northward to pass through the heart of the Marble
Mountains, the trail passes through two wilderness areas that provide some of the finest
backpacking in California. Besides combining the
best of both worlds — the lush vegetation of the
Cascades and the glaciated canyons and alpine
lakes of the Sierra — the Trinitys and the Marbles
offer a singular world of their own design: a botanical wonderland unlike any other along the path.
Due to their unique geologic makeup and the tempering influence of the relatively near Pacific
Ocean on the local climate, these mountains house
several botanical species that are found nowhere
else in the world. Even the common varieties of

flora are thrown together in extraordinary communities: Russian Peak, sandwiched between the two wilderness areas, has 19 species of conifers growing on its slopes.

The terrain was not to be outdone in this display of variety. Roaming between the 1400-2500-foot lowlands of the Sacramento, Salmon and Klamath rivers and the 6500-7800-foot ridgelines of the Trinitys and the Marbles, the trail does a fair imitation of northern Yosemite's "washboard topography." To chase away the washday blues, much of the permanent trail has been routed along ridgecrests, providing sweeping panoramic vistas that would burn out the eyes of the sinner. The grand jumble of distant peaks and ridges looking like a jigsaw puzzle just dumped from its box, alpine lakes of exquisite beauty, playfully gushing streams whose pools cry to be swum in, caves dripped into the cliffsides of the Marbles — it was altogether stunning country.

At the outset of the journey, I gave little thought to homefolks and the homeland. But recent days have seen the road lined with the ripening blackberry bushes of my old backyard. A few evenings ago: a pocket valley with great stands of Douglas-fir clothing its slopes; its floor a lush, seemingly impenetrable, tangle of ferns and shrubbery, hallmark of the Cascades' west slope forests; the evening sun, filtering through the dense forest top, casting a columnar light of eerie excitement, and longing. Another evening, spent working through the journey's paper-schedule to accommodate a trail rendezvous and celebrations in Oregon. I've a touch of the Hearth-and-Home blues centering my roadway meditation, a mantra of memories and anticipation.

The roads have provided their own sap to my spirit; there has been perhaps one day of trail spread thinly over the last week. Rest breaks are short and to the point, more break than rest, for where is the refreshment when one's company is the roaring fumes of mobile castles and trees-on-wheels. The natural-history book has spent a lot of time in the pack ... what pleasure is there in discovering that it is a mountain beaver that lies next to the road, a stinking mat of gore and fly-fodder; what satisfaction in being able to identify the isolated white fir in a Douglas-fir forest when the blue line around its trunk means it will be eliminated by summer's end? Is it any wonder that the camera sees scant activity when its every scene is framed by pavement and telephone poles?

What offense the surfeit of roads did not cause the psyche was directed at the feet. A lifetime of walking sidewalks did not prepare me for how much less resilient a dirt road was than a trail of duff, how much more punishing a paved road was than any other type of hiking surface I encountered. Even a patchy scattering of light gravel atop the pavement would be a palpable relief.

Picture a step: leading with the heel, which absorbs the shock of the body's full weight, sending vibrations up through the fragile, skimpily sheathed Achilles tendon; rolling through the step, skin stretching taut over the ball of the foot, depriving it of all its natural cushion as it momentarily balances all the weight on its point; pushing off the toes, which slide inside the boot to that point of greatest leverage, greatest pressure. On an average day of the trek, each foot would have repeated this process nearly 13,000 times under pack; during the Big Push, as many as 25,000 times. By day's end, feet would be flattened, somewhat swollen. The Achilles tendon would have again swollen tight within its sheath. The ball of my foot would ache with bruises. The nails of my small toes would be just the slightest bit more twisted and contorted than the evening before.

The feet have a fairly unsophisticated means of self-defense: they develop calluses. Coarse thicknesses of skin horseshoed the base of my heel, coated the ball of my foot across its entire width, grew horny shells along the edges of big and small toes. However, not only were the calluses insufficient in coping with the overload of stress to skin and bone, they were self-defeating: this tough, thick growth was like a layer of paving on the foot itself. Pressure blisters developed beneath the calluses of heel and ball and along their leading edges, producing a niggling discomfort and ultrasensitivity to my walking surface.

Eventually, I took to wearing my old running shoes for roadwalking. The lowcut nylon uppers with a wear-hole in each side wouldn't support Jello. But on pavement, support isn't the issue, cushion is. Recently resoled, the running shoes turned the road into a winding ribbon of downy comfort . . . or at least a bed of young thorns.

I leave the dirt road to follow a lesser logging road with no markings: the Forest Service's temporary route. It is a calculated risk. As someone should have once said: calculated risks are only for fools and clairvoyants. The road narrows, the twistings become more intricate. A rusted section marker gives me my position; yellow-orange survey tape along an overgrown logger's path plays the tease. The cal-

culated risk becomes a gamble: I take a bearing and head upslope.

The path disintegrates as timber gives way to dense fields of chaparral. The gods smile on my obsession: instead of manzanita, a shrub of unmatched obstinacy always looking for a stranglehold, my principal obstacle is huckleberry oak, a more densely but more delicately branched shrub than manzanita with a more malleable character. The bushwhack progresses; adrenalin is one of man's more functional gifts. I make for a trailcut but it is just a playful apparition in the setting sun. Hard-won elevation is frivolously tossed away as I use my compass to follow the map of my imagination.

On a jeep road heading up a neighboring ridge, Sol points out a patch of tarnished gold: a section marker on a roadside tree that sets me back on my ancient topo map just an amble or two from a stretch of brand, spanking new trail. My cries of delight chase the sun over its last ridge; the last shreds of this morning's pissin' and moanin' are consumed by the flames of my accomplishment. Castle Crags and Mt. Shasta tip their caps of alpenglow in acknowledgment.

There is a trail guide for the Pacific Crest Trail that is remarkably specific: mileages between landmarks calibrated to the tenth of a mile, elevations given at every trail junction, compass bearings at every turning. It is revised and reissued every couple of years — yet it is still no match for the wildfire spread of the logging plague. During my travels through northern California, I had a copy of the galley proofs for the latest revision of the California guide, which was not published until after I had moved into the Pacific Northwest. Not yet back from the printer, the guide was already outdated in some instances: a jeep-road trail section would be left hanging in the air as a new logging road undercut it; a once-correct turning would lead down a cul-de-sac, bound by piles of freshly harvested forest; beautifully marked new sections of permanent trail that I could follow in my sleep would end abruptly in a spaghetti of logging roads with no sign but tire treads.

There's a story. Jim Bridger and Kit Carson were jawing one time, trading tales, and Jim Bridger asked: "Kit, have you ever been lost?" Kit Carson considered this for a spell, then retorted: "Lost? No, I can't say as I've ever been lost. A mite confused for about a week or so, but never lost." The northern California logging maze was often a mite confusing.

Today I am alone and I revel in my solitude. True, the throaty hum of the logging truck rises early to my ears from the valley 2000 feet below, and four silent spots of humanage are visible on the shores of Lake Helen as I pass above. But they are like flies on a neighbor's dungheap: I am alone. Leaving shorts in the pack, I swing freely along the day's ridgecrest, brushing lingering Mt. Shasta and the nearing Trinity Alps with my wings.

The morning begins with a stretch of cross-country, then trail that only occasionally shows its face. Through creekside meadowlands and woods, nooked and crannied with deer and rabbit, it is slowgoing and delightful. For it is totally involving. In the past I have thought of roads as divorcing me from my sur-

*roundings only because I went encased in steel
and glass. But my experiences with roadwalking have exhibited their own form of sep-
aration, my mind becoming encased in
memories and projections. Several years ago,
after a multi-pitch climb of Cathedral Peak
near Tuolumne Meadows, I was filled with
amazement in listening to the two rope-leaders
discussing the climb. They could recall every
flake, every feldspar nubbin, every bombproof
hold, while I remembered only gross features:
the chimney, the summit pinnacle. But in
leading the climb, in selecting pin placement,
their involvement with the rock had been much
more nearly total than mine.*

*The trail guide offers a safe, sure alterna-
tive route along major logging roads for those
who have found the route-finding process to be
a burden. For me, the more challenging route
has been a blessing. My senses seem sharper,
my appreciation for my surroundings en-
hanced, my enthusiasm and eagerness greater.*

*A brief discourse on the subject of walking.
Three styles of movement have melded into my
journey. There is "walking to": wind-up,
goal-oriented, get-me-to-the-church-on-time
walking. Then there is "walking through," for
people with camera and natural-history books
in their bellypacks. Finally there is simply
"walking," for those who don't believe rhythm
need be confined to the dance floor or the bed-
room, and for whom the sensual pains and
pleasures of movement are an end in themselves.*

*Though each of the first two styles has its
particular adherents, I appear to be the only*

Trailer to champion the cause of the sen-
sualists in the audience. I've not heard another
Trailer mention an enjoyment of backpacking
for the sheer joy of movement. John Barth once
wrote, "The key to the treasure is the treasure,"
but most folks seem to be in it only for the
money.

Marathon hiking is a mutation, a changeling in the family of wilderness experience. There were many degrees of abnormality, however, among those of us following the North Star. The most extreme example was the computerized walkers from the University of Connecticut. The U-Conn Expedition, they called themselves. As I heard it (I never met them), one of their number was a computer-science major who had fed trail variables — time parameters, terrain, water availability, climatic data — into a computer. The computer told them to start hiking north from a point in the northern Sierra, return to that point by motor after reaching Canada, then continue their walk south to Mexico. They carried the printout with them, for it listed each evening's camp spot along with the mileage to be covered that day. I saw a copy of their printout when visiting the trail-guide publishers after the conclusion of my journey. It even had such annotations as what days would include swimming breaks. Artoo-Detoo comes to the wilderness . . . John Muir must be having nightmares in his grave.

Then there were the two fellows from Minnesota. Originally known as the Minnesota Twins, then the Minnesota Milers, and finally as the Minnesota Masochists, they were said to open conversations with the backpackers they met by announcing that they hiked thirty miles a day. And

Strider, who registered a 43-mile day in the central Oregon Cascades. The tales floated back down the grapevine, logged in trail registers as a challenge to those who followed. It is the nature of marathon hiking that many would pick up the gauntlet. This seemed particularly likely of those playing the name-game. The honor of the Street Gang was at stake; the Jets is gonna *make* it, man.

There is a tragic flaw in the goal of hiking from Mexico to Canada in one season: the goal itself. Gaining the end and enjoying the means are nearly mutually exclusive propositions. Trailers who looked more with their eyes than with their feet were not given to "finishing" the trail: Leyton, of the hundred-pound pack, was reported last seen fishing the reservoirs of southern Oregon around Labor Day; the gentle naturalists from UC-Irving — Peter, Pam and Gail — decided early on to scale down their journey, forsaking the complete dinner to dine *a la carte* on the more outstanding offerings of California. Trailers with eyes only for Canada seemed to see little else.

I was fortunate. I managed to mend the gap between process and product. Traveling alone was a useful tool. And my trail journal's demands on my eyes and mind proved a cohesive binder. It was a fragile joining, severely frayed and subject to sudden breakages. Yet it held my journey together.

The trail winds down to a couple miles of state highway and I see my first people in two days, driving by in automobiles and campers. Somehow that seems appropriate, as if someone is trying to tell me, "Listen kid, when we're talking society, we're talking machines." Oh, if only Phil Ochs were alive today . . . what a field day he would have.

I so enjoy hiking in the early evening. The air has cooled and I can experience the sensual pleasures in the contrast of sun and shade, rather than seeking out every forest canopy as a desperate refuge from the sweltering sun of midday. And the deer are out now taking their sup. They always bolt at my approach, spronging out of sight and smell. I try to tell them to pay me no mind, that running off in mid-meal is bad for the digestion, but they never stay long enough to hear.

The last couple of days I've had to bring out the Halazone tablets. The Trinity Alps are not much more than an alpine cow pasture. Now, I've drunk some water on this trip that most folks wouldn't use to wash their cars, and I've been able to walk more often than squat the next day. But really, when a cow's standing there going tail-up in my watering hole, I've got to draw the line.

Water. It was the lead question of everyone I met during the journey, right up there with "What's been your favorite place?" I'm surprised you were so long in asking it.

It was the year of the drought. Shasta Lake, in the Mt. Shasta region of northern California, had received only eight inches of precipitation during the past rain year; its normal is eighty inches. Even springs were drying up. And when the Crest Trail was true to its name, what water there was lay below the trail, often inconveniently so. As with nearly every other facet of the journey, however, I found that my need for water and my impression of its scarcity were matters of perspective.

Although I don't believe that the body appreciably lessens its need for water, regardless of how gradually it is weaned from the bottle, I do know that the demands of the mind can be altered over time. In southern California, which is dry by nature rather than an abnormality of nature, I often carried a gallon of water or more. I was unaware of what my needs were in such conditions and feared the worst. By the time I had reached drought-stricken northern California, I had learned. On one 25-mile waterless stretch near Lassen, for example, I spent most of an afternoon at my last source of water: drinking my fill, eating my evening meal, then drinking some more. In late afternoon, I shouldered my pack and walked through the cool hours of evening until dusk. Morning found me on the trail, drinking in the chill vapors of dawn. By early afternoon, I had reached my next water: I had carried two quarts, had drunk only one and a half. The drought was never a factor for me.

The Salmon River is painted in greens and golds. The deep greens of the pools whose bedrock bottoms seem as close as a whisper; of the lush, vari-toned, vari-textured vegetation of a Cascadian forest floor. The golds of early morning sun flowing over the canyon rim, shimmering, dancing on the stony bed of the shallows; of the sweet siren who lives in these mountains, whose charms are measured by the ounce. It is a river of storied past, a feast for present senses.

I don't stop to visit the cave in Black Mountain's marbled body, as I had planned. Something draws me on, on to the Jumpoff. And there they are, framed in the distance by a notch in the next ridge: the twin peaks of Red Butte. They aren't Oregon, but only a 5½-mile whisker separates the butte from the Home-

land. I'd been tinkering with the notion of pushing into Seiad Valley a day early ... nothing serious, mind you, just idle mind games. Now the spirit cries "Home!" and the body listens. My pace quickens and the miles pass beneath me to settle in the dust. The pollen of trailside greenery spells Home on my sweating skin. And on my knolltop bed, the glistening rays of a setting sun are blown across my face by a northwesterly breeze ... from home.

Good evening, Mr. Grider, sir. I would like to ask for the hand of your creek in marriage.

All sweetness and light, Grider Creek is a Salmon River in miniature. A blend of cascades and pools and fresh greens, I can taste its delight in the very air. And more: roly-poly black bear cubs trundling along the trail. There is a sinister note to their play, however: cubs mean a nearby sow, whose unpredictability in their defense lurks in the dark corners of my consciousness. I wait back awhile for the cubs to take their leave, then return to my tete a tete with Mr. Grider's offspring.

Grider Creek carries the Trailer down out of the Marble Mountains to the grasslands of the Klamath River and Seiad Valley, the last trailside community in California. The stay in the lowlands is a short one, however: in the first six miles out of Seiad Valley, the trail climbs 3700 feet up to the crest of the Siskiyou Mountains.

The Siskiyous are the geologic mate of the Marbles and bear the same proximity to the coast and the tempering influence of its climate. Thus, these mountains too serve as an arboretum *extraordinaire,* making a goulash of the conventional plant communities and painting the open slopes with a rainbow of wildflowers. As I began the near-hundred-mile northeastward swing that would return me to the Cascade range, the Siskiyous presented me with wide-angle panoramas and scant, frequently cattle-polluted water sources. And a state line. After walking for 16 weeks and 1550 miles, I put California behind me and returned to the Pacific Northwest.

The view from Devils Peak is awesome: the Klamath River curling through its valley 4600 feet below, the Marble Mountains beginning their heady rise to the south from its banks. It is a saddening sight though. Over on those hills to the south, you see, Mother E had fashioned a jigsaw puzzle of richly forested slopes. But several of the pieces are missing now; burly young men have come and taken them away. Off to the southwest there, a whole great section is missing. Looks like an entire hillside may have fit in there once. Sort of reminds me of the puzzles I had as a child. They were always losing pieces. A little harder to put together perhaps, but it could still be done. And I could always picture it as it once was when all the pieces were there. But what of the people who come to Devils Peak now, or ten years from now, who have never seen this puzzle with all its pieces intact?

I pass through a grove of knobcone pines. Like the giraffe of the animal community, this is a tree that has been designed by a committee. It combines aspects of fir, pine and a kitchen-utensil rack. I won't quibble with the something-borrowed-something-blue characteristics of its bark, needles and form, but those clumps of cones that grow directly from its trunk and its limbs like some kind of warts are

*the damnedest sight. The tree seems to be say-
ing, "Stare at me if you like, but be proud, for I
am one of God's creations . . . I think."*

*My entry into Oregon is attended by no
fanfare, no slapping of hands or moment of
prayer.*

*Perhaps it is the surroundings: an axe-
ravaged slope, cut and burnt within an inch of
its life. Perhaps it is the lack of markings. I
can't stand solemnly/joyfully/histrionically,
one foot on either side of the line − I have no
idea where the line is. No natural demarcation
here: the state line follows the god-grid that
drops onto my map from the sky.*

*But the crossing is made. I've come home.
The journey rides high on the crest of my quiet
satisfaction.*

Northern California Trail Log

Date	Camp	Elevation	Mileage
July 4	Humboldt Summit area	6490	22
5	Gurnsey Creek Campground	4710	19*
6	Warner Valley Campground	5640	20
7	Cave Campground — supply pick-up in Old Station	4340	27
8	Burney Falls State Park	2920	28
9	Nelson Creek	2600	17*
10	Deer Creek	3100	17*
11	Cabin Creek	2680	15
12	Castle Crags State Park — supply pick-up in Dunsmuir	2160	15
13	Castle Crags area	6200*	12*
14	Toad Lake area	7820	15*
15	Masterson Meadow area	5660	16
16	North Fork Coffee Creek	4800	19
17	Trail Creek Campground	4720	12
18	Mule Bridge camping area	2820	19
19	above Kidder Creek Valley	6320	16
20	Big Ridge	7030	19
21	Seiad Valley — supply pick-up	1370	22
22	Cook and Green Pass	4750	15
23	Donomore Meadows	5800	21
24	Bull Gap area	5960	19

Totals
385 miles
 21 hiking days

California: 1552 miles
 103 hiking days
 9 layover days

*elevations approximate to the nearest 100 feet, mileage approximate to the nearest mile

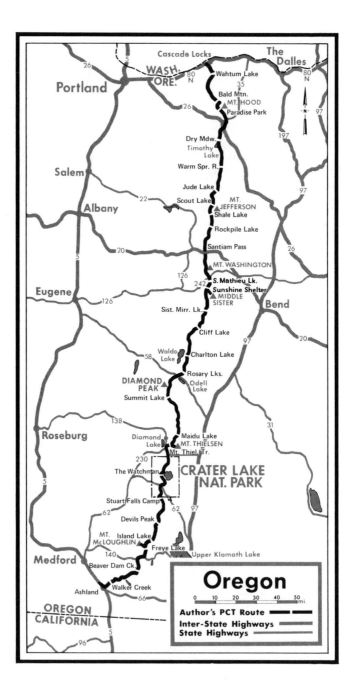

Cascade Locks · The Dalles

WASH.
ORE.

Portland

Wahtum Lake
Bald Mtn.
MT. HOOD
Paradise Park

Dry Mdw.
Timothy Lake
Warm Spr. R.

Jude Lake
Scout Lake · MT. JEFFERSON
Shale Lake
Rockpile Lake

Santiam Pass
MT. WASHINGTON

S. Mathieu Lk.
Sunshine Shelter
MIDDLE SISTER

Sist. Mirr. Lk.

Cliff Lake

Waldo Lake · Charlton Lake

Rosary Lks.
DIAMOND PEAK · Odell Lake
Summit Lake

Maidu Lake
Diamond Lake · MT. THIELSEN
Mt. Thiel. Tr.

The Watchman

Stuart Falls Camp

Devils Peak

MT. McLOUGHLIN · Island Lake
Freye Lake
Upper Klamath Lake

Medford
Beaver Dam Ck.

Ashland · Walker Creek

OREGON
CALIFORNIA

Salem

Albany

Eugene

Bend

Roseburg

CRATER LAKE NAT. PARK

Portland

Oregon

0 10 20 30 40 50 mi.

Author's PCT Route
Inter-State Highways
State Highways

Oregon

*C'mon already, Sol. I've slept at least three
night's worth by now. It's about time you
crossed my face with a little eastern-rim
lighten-up.*

*Finally tiring of waking to a bowlful of
stars spilling into my eyes, I convince myself
that the city-light glow in the northeastern sky
is really God turning on the tap for his morning sun-shower. I'm not far off the mark. And
Ashland is there, stretching out her new-
morning arms to receive me. Let the Celebration begin!*

Dropping out of the Siskiyou Mountains, I spent two days playing tourist in the "civilization preserve" of Ashland. It was my Return to the Homeland celebration: taking in a couple plays at the Oregon Shakespeare Festival, eating in quality and variety as well as in quantity, baring my feet to the caressing grasses of cultivated park lawns, blending the whisper of a summer breeze playing in the big-leaf maples with the more strident sounds of children at play, adding a book on the geology of the major Cascade peaks to my pack's one-volume natural-history library. Two days. It was my first experience with dawn-to-dusk immobility since leaving Yosemite Valley over six weeks earlier. It was not difficult to tear myself away, however. So thoroughly accustomed to movement, I found big chunks of idleness to be enervating. Back in harness, I headed northeastward over two days' worth of parched roadway to rejoin the Cascades.

The Cascades are a range of mixed breeding. There are cinder cones scattered throughout the range, consisting entirely of the fragmented, pyroclastic debris of violent eruptions. The relatively minor peaks — Mts. Washington and Thielsen, and Three-finger Jack — began life as gently sloping shield volcanoes of "quietly" erupting, fluid basalt, though each is now little more than a spike of the more viscous lava that clogged its central vent. Then there are the statuesque stratovolcanoes, the Hoods, Rainiers and Shastas, whose towering cones are layer cakes of pyroclastic debris and evenly flowing lavas. They have undergone the rack of orogenic uplift and a continuous cycle of eruption — the Cascade volcanoes are considered only dormant, not extinct, and Mts. Baker,

Rainier, St. Helens, Hood, Shasta and Lassen have all been active within the last 150 years — and have been subjected to the ravenous jaws of as many as four major glaciations as well as ongoing consumption by present-day alpine glaciers. The stratovolcanoes are mere babes, still at the tender age of a million years or less. Towering, majestic, they ride on the rolling hills of their elders. For beneath the hot, young bucks of the major peaks lie great interbedded thicknesses — as much as six miles in places — of basaltic lava flows, mudflows, volcanic ash, and rock compacted from volcanic sediments, whose origins extend back forty million years and more. It is this ancient volcanic rock, spotted with subsurface granitic intrusions, that gives the Cascades their breadth of 30-50 miles.

In the Oregon Cascades the Crest Trail begins at the foot of 9493-foot Mt. McLoughlin, southern Oregon's only remaining stratovolcano peak. An early morning scramble up McLoughlin served as a prelude to my entry into the Sky Lakes area, a land thickly forested with fir, pine and hemlock, pocketed with secluded woodland lakes and imbued with the enchantment of elves and wood sprites. Although the Crest Trail generally follows the route of the Oregon Skyline Trail through the Cascades, they often part ways in the Sky Lakes area, the Skyline Trail meandering through lake basins while the Crest Trail hugs the forested, waterless crest. I sampled a bit of both worlds before treading the pumice flats of the Oregon Desert, with its sparse covering of lodgepole pine, on my way to Crater Lake National Park.

I stop in at the Big Elk forest service station to chat for a bit with the two young folks tending house there for the summer. One asks what

I have seen in the way of wildlife. I begin by mentioning the multitude of deer ... "Oh, deer don't count," he interjects, "they're everywhere; we've got 'em camping in our backyard." Familarity breeding contempt? They haven't been here but a month ... how quickly we become jaded.

Climbing the sun, with Mt. McLoughlin as my ladder. There's a trail to the top but it's a bit like walking up a down escalator, the finely ground volcanic rock slipping away beneath me like the silvery balls of a mercury maze. I celebrate the sun and summit with nectarines and plums, given me by the two folks who shared the mountaintop with the full moon. My eyes partake of a separate feast: Mt. Shasta glowing in the south, its snowcap a sun unto itself ... the southern rim of Crater Lake pricking the northern horizon, with two of the Sisters taking a peek at my world from behind Mt. Thielsen's shoulder ... the glassy sheets of Fish Lake, Four Mile Lake, Lake O'the Woods, all flawless mirrors in the forest lawn.

Woodland lakes are not so wildly beautiful as their alpine cousins, but they have a placid, restful nature that is a balm to the spirit. If you are one of the blessed, you will discover Marguerette, Queen of the Sky Lakes. Deep and clear, she'll charm you with her bluesy-greens and rock you to sleep in the arms of an afternoon breeze. And filling your head with memories of her cliffside beauty, she'll waft you back up to the ridgecrest, where Luther Mountain stands as a singular jewel in her crown.

The author and equipment at home in Portland—neither he nor his gear would ever be this clean again. (photo by Saralie Northam)

The Mexican border—a stretch of barbed wire, a lone trail sign, a first step.

A hoary limber pine growing beneath the summit of Mt. Baden-Powell in the San Gabriel Mountains.

Mormon Rocks, in the canyoned gap between the San Bernardino and the San Gabriel mountains—they have ridden the movement along the San Andreas fault for miles from their birthplace.

Joshua tree along the Old Sierra Highway in the western Mojave Desert—unique to the high deserts of the southwest, it looks like some vegetative orangutan.

The Kern River Canyon at Grasshopper Flat—"The Kern River Trail [was] my stairway to the gods."

Author and faithful hiking staff atop Mt. Whitney—"Mists rise from the netherworld to pay homage to the Mountain King."
(photo by Rich Little)

The barren plateau below Forester Pass, high point along the PCT—"As the walls . . . funnel me towards the pass, the richocheting wind plays me like a pinball wizard."

The onset of spring in the high country—Lake Helen begins to thaw beneath a shoulder of Black Giant, near Muir Pass in the High Sierra.

In late May, this is the path least traveled by: the John Muir Trail, heading up through Upper Basin to Mather Pass.

The tranquility of early morning—Benson Lake in the Yosemite backcountry.

The Quintessential Sierran Tarn—"water so clear that I was knee-deep before I realized I'd broken the surface."

Summer afternoon thunderstorm threatens Sierra Buttes in the northern Sierra.

The knifecraft of the Basque sheepherder on the "canvas" of a lodgepole pine, White Canyon near Sonora Pass in the northern Sierra.

Sun and stream, dancing a delicate *pas de deux* at Tangle Blue Creek in the Trinity Alps of northern California.

Bigelow sneezeweed: the radiance of this member of the sunflower family makes a mockery of its name.

Evening settles on the High Siskiyous as the Oregon-boy approaches his homeland.

The author at Crater Lake, with Wizard Island rising from its waters—"I approach the lake as a lover. . . . Gently, she takes me in indigo arms, takes my sweat and my pain and my exuberance, and leaves me limp in the embrace of afterglow."

". . . the afternoon cannonade begins in the greying west and the full screen reflection of Mt. Jefferson in Shale Lake is first dimpled, then shattered, by the occasional sprinkle . . ."

Author atop Middle Sister in the Oregon Cascades, South Sister in the background—"Up and up and up I climb, till the moment when there is no more Up and the sky rushes in to meet me at every turn."

"From timberline, Mt. Adams stands to reveal itself. What a massive, overwhelming presence! With what broad strokes the Master Artist created this work!"

Reflection pool in the Washington Cascades, above Chinook Pass near Mt. Rainier National Park.

Three Fools Peak in the North Cascades near the Canadian border--"A striking scene, worn by my eyes as a laurel wreath by the victor. It is an acutely personal triumph, for only I know the game that has been played these several months."

Leaving Glacier Peak Wilderness after an early autumn storm—
"Fir trees, pregnant with snowchild, sway heavily in the gilding
sun."

There I am. Just sittin' atop Devils Peak, not a care in the world. Peaklets and lake basins aswirl at my feet and Mt. McLoughlin an easel to the evening sun. Belly full and mind afloat. Then the sun sets, bed is laid, and the mosquitos join the dance. Mosquitos? What the hell? Closest water is a thousand feet below me; the peak here is dry as death. But truth pays little heed to reason. So it goes. The close harmony of skeeter serenade sifts in through my shuttered ears. Comfort scorning appearances, the tent goes up on my small, sandy platform and the rest comes easy.

For many people, whether they look at it in a picturebook or through the camera viewfinder, Crater Lake is only a picture, a reason to stop the car and stretch the legs, a place to sticker to their bumper. But when one has walked nearly 1700 miles . . .

I round a bend in the road and there lies the rim before me. Exultation wells up through my body, erupting in cinder cones of emotion at every pore, the debris of enthrallment. The intensity of my response is almost erotic. I approach the lake as a lover, reaching into the clouds for downy linens. Gently, she takes me in indigo arms, takes my sweat and my pains and my exuberance, and leaves me limp in the embrace of afterglow.

Crater Lake. Once it was a vast, sprawling volcano, perhaps 12,000 feet in height, its slopes fuming with parasitic cinder cones and lava-spewing fissures. Until 6600 years ago. Then, with a hellish, consumptive roar, it disgorged some fifteen cubic miles of its innards and collapsed in upon itself. Its smoking caldera, 4000 feet deep and five to six miles across, quieted with time, then gradually filled with the waters of snowmelt and rain to form an alpine lake of such Junoesque proportions and consummate beauty that it beggars the senses.

I had been to Crater Lake before. It was not cloaked in mystery. My approach was not steeped with anticipation. It was early August, the height of the tourist crush. The rim road was an endless stream of exhaust and Winnebago-whine. Yet despite my familarity, despite my lack of a private moment, my Crater Lake experience was the emotional peak of the journey. When I awoke the next morning, I was so thoroughly drained I could hardly move.

Crater Lake was also an experience of the backpacker as an anarchic microcosm. If I did have one expectation regarding Crater Lake, it was that I would spend a night atop one of the rim peaks. I inquired at Park Headquarters and my request was summarily dismissed. After months on the trail, however, I had come of a feeling of absolute independence, of responsibility to no one but myself. To sleep atop Garfield, atop the Watchman, would be a victimless crime. I suffered only slight hesitation and nary a pang of guilt as I set my bed on a slat bench of the Watchman's observation tower. From nearly 2000 feet above the lake's surface. I viewed the rise and fall of Sol and Luna, and admired the clouds knit by the fiery needles of an electrical storm over southern Oregon.

From Crater Lake, I began a three-week, 325-mile trek northward along the spine of the Oregon Cascades and its string of wilderness areas: Diamond Peak, Three Sisters, Mt. Washington, Mt. Jefferson, Mt. Hood. It was quite literally a crest trail now, tightroping the ridgeline between east and west slopes, passing just beneath the summits of the major peaks, the milestones of the Crest Trail in Oregon. As I progressed along the trail there was a feeling of movement even in their stillness, as the big peaks appeared to near, pass by in review, then recede into the past. Yesterday's north became tomorrow's south. The trail's builders had artfully mixed dense stands of forest intimacy with full frontal close-ups and middle distance exposures of whatever peaks were on the day's menu. The Three Sisters Wilderness went even further in providing environmental variety: its southern portion is freckled with cool woodland lakes and lily ponds; as one steps out from the shadow of the closely bunched trio of 10,000-foot Sisters in its northern sector, s/he is confronted with great spreads of lava flows, some as young as 1500 years — geological infants.

I climbed Mt. Thielsen and Middle Sister more for the summits' exhilarating and energizing effect than for the expansive views. Vistas were clouded by the smoky residue of August forest fires and field burning in the Willamette Valley, Oregon's agriculture and population trough that parallels the Cascades to the west. Here in the Land of Perpetual Rain, where moss grows even on the rolling stones and space-age plastics turn to rust, the drought had still managed to establish itself. The evening electrical storm I had witnessed from the Watchman had sparked nearly a dozen and a half fires. Two days later, the bans were announced: no backcountry fires allowed in the Oregon Cascades. This was a restriction I readily respected and observed, but then I am not a Firemaker by nature. Except for the small stickfires I used for cooking in the Sierra when my stove was on the fritz, I turned my evening gaze to the stars rather than the dancing flame. The night sky proved an able choreographer, the summer months being ripe with meteor showers.

The Indians of the Pacific Northwest believed great spirits lived at the tops of the mountains. Those few Indians who would risk angering the spirits by venturing to the mountain heights were seen by their tribespeople as gaining greater energy, strength and spirit. To visit the mountain spirits was to acquire the power of spirits.

I sit in early sun, in the parlor of the spirits of Thielsen. The Indian belief is not such a heathen one, I think. I drink of Thielsen's strength, riding the wings of the eagle. Yet I wonder what the hell kind of Mountain King would live in the form of the golden-mantled ground squirrel that's holding such serious conversations with the bag of dried fruit and granola at my side.

Maidu Lake

Beneath the mists of morning
Rippling circles grow.
The trout are feeding.

I pull around the northeast spur of Diamond Peak and catch sight of the Sisters. They have changed since yesterday; they are so much closer now. I can reach out and . . . touch, almost. The effect is electric. My expectations for a lazy day drain away through the porous volcanic rock. I catch the rhythm and begin to move, the miles of trail clicking away beneath my rolling feet like so much steel rail. This train's bound for glory.

I stop awhile at my lazy day's intended camp, now reached in early afternoon. It is a beautiful little lake, deep and sparkling, with a spur of the Diamond visible above its far shore. It works its magic well and I pause to play porpoise and the idle-rich for some time. But the magic of mountains is a potent force. The lodestone of the Sisters draws me on, the strength of Thielsen's spirit flowing through my body.

Old Sol calls in sick this morning, saying he may be in later. But by midday, strange squeaks and groans are coming from the woodwind section, pitchpipe of the ancients, as Mother E strikes up a lively breeze. Overhead, Rip Van Winkle's cohorts gather for a Sunday afternoon of duckpins on the green. Displaying appreciable skill, I might add. From a rocky bluff, I watch the storm donner and blitz above Waldo Lake to the west, lighting a fire on the far shore, then dousing the flames as it lays its watery tribute at my feet.

Last evening closed with great clots of multi-greys layering awkwardly overhead like the ill-wrought strokes of a novice in oils. The morning's first sun, however, paints Charlton Lake as a delicate still life, the shoreside fireweed glowing embers of pink translucence. The forest is strangely quiet. When the muffled thud of my step comes to a halt, the silence is absolute. The drone of insect breath is more felt than heard. A trickle of early morning sunstreams filters through the forest canopy. I walk on, cloaked in spiderstrands of silver, through the enchanted forest.

I knew the Sisters would be barren and not the young lovelies of my memories. Still, it is a shock to see what weather-beaten old hags they've become after the lean winter. A few tattered glacial rags are all that is left to adorn themselves with. There is revelation in their nakedness though. Like a deer that's been felled by the cat, great gouts of flesh have been torn from their sides by ancient glaciers, exposing raw, red rock beneath their grey, slag-heap hides.

Up and up and up I climb, till the moment when there is no more Up and the sky rushes in to meet me at every turn. Every summit holds a mirror up to the climber, the looking glass of reward. Middle Sister replaces my customary summit reaction of electric thrill with a warm numbness, due perhaps to the sandblasting effect of the 40-50 mph east wind.

The descent, too, provides a novel experience after the initial quick-and-dirty, shoe-filling scree run carries me on to the bouldery western spur. There, crisscrossing the line between weightiness and weightlessness, my descent is, like skiing, a controlled fall. The feet have eyes and move as magic wands to keep the body upright. The mind is put on hold; its deliberateness would only interfere as legs flit me down the mountain, creating a vibrant pas de deux *of rock and man.*

At Santiam Pass, in the central Oregon Cascades, a vanguard of homefolks whisked me off into the lap of luxury at a mountain condominium for a weekend of forced idleness and near-painful amounts of food.

I had been apprehensive about the rendezvous. My contact with homefolks during the journey had been slight: regular phone-checks with the friends coordinating my supply packages; an occasional letter received and responded to. I produced a monthly article in a local newspaper, excerpted from my trail journal, to tell of my whereabouts and how-did-I-do's. It was a comfortable detachment, undemanding. My trail contacts, too, had called for little investment. Immediate, momentary, ships-passing-in-the-night engagements. For over four months, I had been a person without a past, my identity a skeleton key that would fit any lock. Approaching this weekend reunion, though, I had been unsure which David would blend into the mesh of old relationships. My anticipation held all the thrill and horror of a blind date. The weekend passed pleasantly, however. Too pleasantly in a way, as a long-lost ladyfriend mysteriously appeared to cement me quite solidly to my past. As I headed into the Mt. Jefferson Wilderness, I was two days talking it through with certain trees that looked particularly understanding before I was able to coax my spirit back into the mountains.

The Mt. Jefferson Wilderness was also the scene of an intriguing contrast in water availability: while water-table streams and springs were everywhere going dry, the torrid heat of mid-August set glacier-fed Russell Creek on such a rampage it required a cautious wading to cross it. Thinking back on the thin snow year, I sat on the bank of this roisterous torrent beneath Jeff's lofty spire and watched as the snows of centuries past flowed to the sea.

The days around Mt. Jefferson are summer-slow and lazy. With this ambling pace comes a feeling of living in the mountains rather than passing through them, a feeling of solidity and entrenchedness, as though I own my evening view lot rather than merely rent it. But the neighborhood's getting crowded. As the afternoon cannonade begins in the greying west and the full screen reflection of Mt. Jefferson in Shale Lake is first dimpled, then shattered, by the occasional sprinkle, the lakeside population rises to 15 for the night.

The early morning sun on heavy dew creates a playground of gold and silver. From atop Jefferson Park ridge, the alpine meadow of Jefferson Park is a great green carpet in the Hall of the Mountain King. Jeff rises abruptly, massively, awesomely from the Park's border, an entity of singular immensity. I am overwhelmed, awash in a feeling of unworthiness, as though coming unclean into the temple.

Beyond Olallie Lake the trail carries me smooth and easy, and the setting sun turns everything my eye touches to gold. Jude Lake is only a half mile from a road yet it is quiet, empty of other people. It has been 10 nights since I was last unaccompanied. I sit on the wooded shore, filling my ears with the wind. The water striders are a ballet, their weightless perfection tickling the lake surface like a gentle rain. A few puffs of cloud are pinked about the edges to lend color to the set. The performance has a somnolent effect, and the audience of one leaves at intermission to go home to bed.

Getting Away from it All! The rallying cry of the Backpacker Nation. And it has become a nation, with communities springing up all along its major thoroughfares. At journey's end, I would look back on my time in Oregon and Washington to find that I *not once* managed to put together two consecutive nights alone with a peopleless day in between. Ocassionally I would begrudge the company — children, particularly Boy Scouts, seem to have a divine imperative to rattle the introspective mirror of a back-country lake with a hail of stones — yet I discovered with time that isolation is measured in the mind more than in space. Several months of mountaining tempered my need for absolutes, trained me in the art of creating seclusion from the materials at hand.

One tool of the craft is the forest. Close and sheltering, it hides all. One common Trailer commentary on the Oregon section of the trail was that "It's okay, if you like looking at lodgepole pines." For these Trailers, the path between Mt. Jefferson and Mt. Hood was perhaps the worst offender. For over 50 miles, there is a little to be seen but the cluttered tangle of an Oregon forest. However, the Trailer complaint does not give it its due: joining the lodgepole is a grand mix of western white pine, red and Alaska cedar, grand, noble, silver and subalpine fir, western and mountain hemlock and Douglas fir.

And if the forest weren't enough, the advent of the Oregon rains with their clinging mists fostered an air of seclusion. It was only drizzle and fog drip at first, breaking for a day or two as I surfaced above timberline on the slopes of 11,235-foot Mt. Hood. The weather held off for my passage along the mountain's west slope, allowing for a pleasant reunion with Dinah, last seen near Mt. Whitney in the southern Sierra; she was my first Trailer encounter in two months. North of Mt. Hood, however, the rains returned, with unexpected vigor, to usher me down Eagle Creek to the Columbia River and Oregon's End.

When the trail presents only viewless forest, one must look to the forest for the views. It is like walking through a cathedral, with great wooden beams rising to the airy arches of foliage above. In some sections the pews of decaying windfall and ancient trail-cut are filled with the congregants: huckleberry and Oregon grape, azalea and rhododendron, vanilla leaf and vine maple. In other areas they lie empty, revealing the thick carpeting of moss. Up close, the grey and crumbling pews have the musty smell of cellar storerooms, keepers of life as new growth feeds on the carcass of the old. The simplicity, the divine rightness of the forest life cycle, enhances my feelings of reverence.

A raindrop hits the mosquito netting, sending a fine spray down into the tent. I wake to angels dancing on my face. There is a giggly, hide-and-seek feeling to being cozily wrapped in the gentle drumming of rain on tent. Each middle-night turning wakes me for a short game. Morning brings stillness and fog drip. A forest walk through the gauzy shroud of low clouds is the ultimate in wilderness intimacy. When Sol finds a slight opening, freckling the forest with his rays, it is as a brash outsider breaking in on our tête á tête. Wispy fingers of mist snatch whole trees away from in front of my face, revealing a huckleberry patch in its stead. Mother E is quicker than the eye.

He is an odd sight walking up the trail at me, brown terry-cloth towel drawn taut over his head as a jury-rigged tumpline. "Where are you coming from?" he asks in a soft voice of the

South. "South a ways," I reply, as I rarely immediately own to starting at the Mexican border unless I'm feeling manipulative. "Campo?" he ventures, a small smile curling up from inside to play briefly about his lips. My astonishment is unaffected.

Bill Foster hiked the Pacific Crest Trail over the summers of 1971 and '72 and he has been walking pret'near ever since. Now on his most ambitious undertaking, he will walk the Crest Trail south until the winter snows drive him down to the great desert east of the Sierra; from Mexico, he will traverse the southern United States to Georgia, from where the Appalachian Trial will carry him north to Maine. His is an unserried tour, with no postal schedules or seasonal time parameters; his is the path of least resistance. He is a romantic, is Bill Foster, a poet by nature if not by trade. We talk of walking and we talk of home, until the chill of the forest shade sets in and we walk on.

It is huckleberry season. I spend endless minutes picking over a few bushes, sating taste and tummy, then move on. A moment later, a particularly succulent berry will peer up at me with a merry eye and cry joyfully, "eat me, please, you must eat me." The exhortation sends a shiver of pleasure up my tongue; I am helpless and must respond. And so the day goes, till the cumulative acid of several quarts of berries forces a hiatus long enough for me to tie a few miles together, trumpeting my presence to those that might follow.

To provide a sense of being transported through time countless millenia into the past, there is no place the equal of the Columbia

River gorge. With low clouds mingling among the surface mists, Wahtum Lake looks like the playground of the Brontosaurus more than the backpacker. Rock encrusted with moss, trees dripping lichen, the fecund understory of the forest, the ever-shadowed defile of Eagle Creek, give a sense of agedness/agelessness. The new rain brings extraordinary richness to the surroundings. It is difficult to gauge the stronger pull: the beauty of Eagle Creek or the home-ing of Portland. I reach the Columbia River, a powerfully tangible line between past and future. Oregon becomes memory; Washington remains as fantasy.

Oregon Trail Log

Date	Camp	Elevation	Mileage
July 25-6	Ashland — Supply pick-up/layover	2000	11
27	Walker Creek	2420	8
28	Beaver Dam Creek	4530	19
29	Freye Lake	6230	16
30	Island Lake — Mt. McLoughlin climb	5960	10
31	Devils Peak	7580	14
Aug 1	Stuart Falls Camp	5590	17
2	The Watchman — supply pick-up at Crater Lake	8060	19
3	Mt. Thielsen Trail junction	7000*	21
4	Maidu Lake — Mt. Thielsen climb	5980	12
5	Summit Lake	5580	23
6	Middle Rosary Lake	5830	25
7	Charlton Lake	5700	14
8	Cliff Lake	5140	19
9	Sisters Mirror Lake	6000	15
10	Sunshine Shelter	6370	14
11	South Matthieu Lake — Middle Sister climb	6040	7
12-4	Santiam Pass area — supply pick-up/layover	3360	22
15	Rockpile Lake	6250	14
16	Shale Lake	5910	9
17	Scout Lake	5810	11
18	Jude Lake	4600	17
19	Warm Springs River	3330	17
20	Dry Meadow area	3840	19
21	Paradise Park shelter	5730	20
22	Bald Mt. area	4270	11
23	Wahtum Lake	3750	20
24-7	Portland — supply pick-up/layover	170	16

Totals

440 miles
28 hiking days
8 layover days

*elevation approximate to the nearest 100 feet.

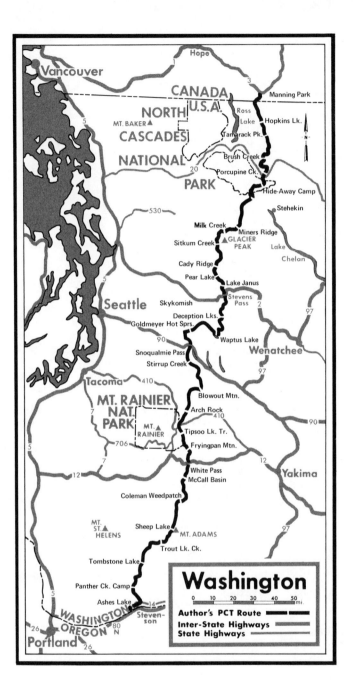

Hope

1

CANADA

3

Manning Park

U.S.A.

NORTH

Ross
Lake

Hopkins Lk.

Vancouver

MT. BAKER▲

CASCADES

Tamarack Pk.

N

NATIONAL

Brush Creek

20

Porcupine Ck.

PARK

Hide-Away Camp

530

Stehekin

Milk Creek

Miners Ridge

Sitkum Creek

▲GLACIER
PEAK

Lake

Cady Ridge

Chelan

Pear Lake

Seattle

Lake Janus

Skykomish

Stevens
Pass

2

97

Deception Lks.

Goldmeyer Hot Sprs.

90

Waptus Lake

Wenatchee

Snoqualmie Pass

Stirrup Creek

97

Tacoma

410

Blowout Mtn.

MT. RAINIER
NAT.
PARK

Arch Rock

410

90

7

MT.▲
RAINIER

Tipsoo Lk. Tr.

5

706

Fryingpan Mtn.

12

7

White Pass

12

McCall Basin

Yakima

Coleman Weedpatch

MT.▲
ST.
HELENS

Sheep Lake

MT. ADAMS

97

Trout Lk. Ck.

Tombstone Lake

Washington

Panther Ck. Camp

0 10 20 30 40 50
mi.

Ashes Lake

14

Author's PCT Route

WASHINGTON

Steven-
son

Inter-State Highways

26

OREGON

80
N

State Highways

Portland

26

Washington

Four days were spent in Portland, replenishing pack and body. It was like Thanksgiving: gathering with friends for four days of gluttony and sloth; supplanting the traditional football rivalries with an afternoon at the soccer stadium, watching Pele and the Cosmos in the championship game. And, as at Thanksgiving, I faced vacation's end with dread, returned to my "work" with reluctance. For the record high temperatures of early and mid-August were being washed away by record rainfalls. As I walked across the Bridge of the Gods over the Columbia River on the last Sunday evening of August, I was escorted by a rare misty lull in the nearly continuous rains.

Although I did not suffer the same despondency that had accompanied the conclusion of the High Sierra, I was again the victim of my expectations. Washington was betraying me. I had envisioned the bracing chill of frosted mornings warming to shirtless afternoons, the hillsides aflame with the colors of aging vine maple and huckleberry bush, the long shadows and golden tones of the autumn sun. Washington was supposed to be gravy, an idle stroll through a fir-lined Eden. Instead, it was the Flood. My second morning, after several hours of torrential rains, I woke to find myself lost in a fog... inside my tent! The dampness was all-pervasive. Even clothing that had been sheltered began to cling with a galling clamminess. Each day found down bag and clothing less lofty, straining less vigorously at the confines of their stuff sacks. It was ugly weather, graceless and without charm.

For nearly five months, the Pacific Crest had been weather-blessed. For the mountain traveler, drought conditions provide a benign environment. Except for the early May storms in the Sierra and, to a lesser degree, the early June storms, the trek had suffered only a very occasional sprinkle. And I had been doubly blessed. I seemed always to walk the edges of the weather. When the High Sierra received two feet of snow and more, I was in the Piutes where less than a foot fell. Although others walked through the customary oppressive, near-100° temperatures in the northern California lowlands, I met only the breezy days of a momentary lapse in the norm. I almost felt like I was cheating.

The Northwest, however, was returning to form, playing proctor on my Pacific Crest exam. I had lived five years in Oregon, was well aware of the stamina and stability of its rains. When Mt.

Adams peeked coyly from behind a veil of disintegrating clouds, I knew it was only a ruse. Even as I walked a second day alongside Adams, the horizon bristling with the spires of Mts. Rainier, St. Helens and Hood, I could not completely shake the undercurrent of urgency that had joined my journey. I no longer trusted in the powers of Sol; I had entered the kingdom of the Storm King. Washington was an impressive display of his ascendancy.

As my months of supportive weather came to an end in Washington, so too did my weeks of companionless hiking. The Trailer parade had begun with a staggered start and its members had continued through the summer at varying speeds. To reach Canada by late September, however, seemed a common goal and, as the autumnal equinox approached, the parade began to close ranks. Near Mt. Adams I met Tim and Tom, two midwestern Trailers whose daily 20-mile gallops had made up for their late April start. They told me of seven more Trailers within two days to my rear. When we arrived at White Pass, the first of the three ski resorts in Washington which have grown up around the summits of the major trans-Cascade highways, there were five other Trailers there to greet us. Although I would manage to find another week for myself above White Pass and a few days of solitude north of Stevens Pass, the feeling of independence that I had gloried in since Lake Tahoe had vanished.

From deep within the forest I can see the mass of brilliant white cutting into the backdrop of cirrus-ed blue. No form or delineation, just a gleaming promise to start the blood perking. As I climb up through the thinner growths, the mass begins to take shape,

*teasing me with partial exposures of the sum-
mit crown. Mainlining adrenalin now brings
the blood to boil . . . . I want to hold that
great motherin' white giant in the palm of my
eye. Awww, Mother E, it feels so good to be
excited again. From timberline, Mt. Adams
stands to reveal itself. What a massive, overwhelming presence! With what broad strokes
the Master Artist created this work! I pay obei-
sance to its majesty, then turn the blood down
to simmer and grab a small bite to eat.*

*Under shredded greys and splotches of
summer we walk, through fields heavy with
the most plump, luscious huckleberries that
the trail has yet offered. As we climb into the
high country, the clouds climb with us, revealing the magnificent sweep of glaciated Klickitat Canyon, the ancient rubble of the Goat
Rocks. Midafternoon, and we huddle inside
the Yelverton Shelter on the slopes of Old
Snowy, the clouds coming back down to us,
hustling before a growing wind. The word
yesterday was of a front moving in from
Alaska; the thought of negotiating the extreme
exposures of the Goat Rocks in the weather it
would bring is not an appealing one. We push
on, the inclemency of the weather growing in
proportion to the sublime beauty of the country.
Snow Creek Canyon falls away 3000 feet below
us as we traverse above the gaping crevasses of
the Packwood Glacier, encountering a party of
horsepackers who had nearly lost an animal to
this tightrope of a trail. We creep along a
knife-edge ridge, the wind accelerating, its
gusts transforming one's rhythmic pace into
the herkyjerk of puppets. The clouds lower still*

more, enfolding us in storm, flaying us with a stinging rain. The shelter of McCall Basin rises to meet us, and the beauty and savagery of the day are steeped in the warmth of evening reflection.

The rain continues unabated through the night. I wake in the morning, a Pooh with his provisions at sea in the flood: an ill-conceived choice of campsites has set my tent in the middle of an overnight pond.

Midday, and a cheerful "howdy-do" to a backcountry ranger brings the response, "you must be hiking the Crest Trail from Mexico." His ambiguous "There's a certain look about you" couldn't have referred to the three of us hiking the rainswept, wind-whipped, open slopes in our shorts, could it?

The Cascades of Washington seem at first to be a continuation of the Oregon range: trail winding through the understory of huckleberry beneath the conifer canopy, meeting the sky only at a cluster of woodland lakes or the occasional patch of clearcut, rolling up through the hill country to the subalpine meadows at the foot of an Adams or a St. Helens. The Goat Rocks provide the first evidence that, though geologically mated with the Cascades of Oregon, the Washington Cascades are a breed apart. Remnant of an ancient stratovolcano that has suffered the ravages of nature's forces over the past two million years of its dormancy, the Goat Rocks area is a country of sinuous alpine ridges rising above severely glaciated canyons.

North of the Goat Rocks, north of civilization's outpost at White Pass, the central Washington Cascades begin to assert their true character. Subject to considerable prehistoric glaciation, due to their more northerly position, the Cascades here are a broader, more strenuously sculpted range. The boggy, horse-trod trail climbs quickly out of the heavy forests to meander along a narrow ridgecrest. Ice-scoured basins drop off on every side to fall away down great, U-shaped troughs. The trail skirts 14,410-foot Mt. Rainier's eastern flank, then leaves it behind to skip windily through the place-names of old mining country — Sourdough Gap, Placer Lake, Pickhandle Point, Bullion Basin.

As clothes and equipment were hung up before the heaters of a rented room at White Pass, the skies cleared. The Storm King granted me a reprieve, lasting nine days. In the midst of this period of grace, however, he sent down a day of whirling clouds and a night of sleet and snow, lest I forget his sovereignty.

Mt. Rainier appears in princely garments, crown of lenticular cloud, robes of silver icefall. I am a pilgrim come before the mountain that was God. My devotions are a peaceful practice, a brimming of quiet joy. Not that exhilaration would be blasphemous ... simply an insufficient expression, like pissing in the ocean. The sun cuts several notches in its belt as I gaze beatific on Takhoma.

Excitement is a chameleon, changing its colors to fit the mood. Morning greets me with the first snow of the fall and my excitement has a crazyquilt of emotions to ride: relief that this latest storm came and went in the night that I spent in the sheltering confines of one of the infrequent trail cabins, anxiety about the three weeks of potential snows that lie ahead, the fever of youth that comes with cracklin-cool air

*and the gilding of firs in new-morning sun.
Through lichened forest, an elk family leads
me down to a golden meadow, where I stay the
morning to watch the earth's vaporous breath
rise, a devotion to the sun.*

*The day begins innocently enough: a skyful
of sun, frosted mummybag, a cluster of elk
ushering me onto the morning trail. Then I
come to the clearcut. I'd heard there was a long
stretch of logging activity ahead but hadn't
given it a second thought. After all, I'm from
Oregon – Home of the Clearcut. But I am not
prepared . . .*

*It is a battlefield, a slaughterhouse opera-
tion of total devastation. I search the vegetable
rubble for signs of life but there is little more
than the incessant honking and accelerative
roar of mechanical parasites. It is so huge; not
the patchwork quilting of Oregon's clearcutting, but giant swaths of now-barren slopes
measurable in miles. One would think Oregon's loggers had cardboard chains in their
saws by comparison. Mt. Rainier peeks over a
ridge, Carbon Glacier a cascade of frozen tears
as the Mountain King watches helplessly over
the mutilation of his domain. I am shaken to
my core. I begin to cry, briefly, quietly; there is
no wailing wall in a clearcut. By the time the
logging road "trail" returns me to the forest,
I've applied an anesthetic to my spirit. Softly
whistling Rod Stewart's "Gasoline Alley," I
slip back into the wilderness.*

Beyond the span of clearcutting, the trail tum-
bles down to the second of its highway/ski resort
complexes, at Snoqualmie Pass. As I climbed into
the Alpine Lakes Wilderness north of the pass, I

left the tragedy of the logging behind: the remaining 250 miles of the trail would pass through a near-continuous string of three wilderness areas and a national park. I also left behind the solely volcanic make-up of the Cascade range. Up to Snoqualmie Pass, the Washington Cascades had differed from the Oregon Cascades only in the eye of the aesthete; now they underwent a change in the eye of the geologist. For Snoqualmie Pass marks the southern border of the North Cascades, a distinct geologic province in which intruded batholiths of granitic rock and a wide range of highly metamorphosed sedimentary rock have been added to the customary surface of young volcanics.

Whether it was due to the more complex geologic realm or simple cussedness, the ridge-and-canyon topography in the Alpine Lakes area became increasingly rugged. Previously, the trail had been able to follow an earthen ridgecrest at a relatively constant elevation. Here, however, the ridges were capped with rocky outcroppings, and the trail was routed from ridge to canyon bottom and back again. The first canyon held the course of the Middle Fork of the Snoqualmie River and a delightful hot spring, whose pool lay inside a cliffside cave. Then the wilderness area began to live up to its name, and every canyon, every alpine meadow, every glacial cirque, housed a pool to mirror the heavens.

It has been a day for the senses . . . merry giggle of a recently dry trailside waterfall as it splashes through the mossy beard of its precipice . . . brilliant sheen of sunspeckled Snow Lake cradled in its rocky cirque . . . foaming fingers of Rock Creek as it bumptiously cascades 2400 feet into the canyon of the Snoqualmie River's middle fork . . . velvet softness of a north-slope forest floor done entirely in the tender greens of mosses and young ferns . . . h'wishing gentleness of aspen-arbored, canyon bottom trail . . . puckering sweetness of the late-season huckleberry . . . oriental delicacy of a mountain scene knife-scratched onto a broad white fungus by a hot springs woman . . . prickly, penetrating warmth of the hot springs tub, reading to worn muscles from the picturebook of youth and melting the day into memories, memories that flicker and fade in an evening campfire.

As the day creeps over the hilltops, the night fights to keep its hold. What are these lightless blotches erasing the fading stars? The wind tosses fitfully in its sleep, moving these unexpected light blots about like chess pieces. The trees bend to converse in low tones and quiet the occasional noisome beastie – "Hush, small one, there's a storm coming." The birds all seem to be walking to work. Within the hour I am enfolded in white and put my eyes back in the pack – visibility is rarely greater than fifty yards. I move swiftly, silently, through clinging mists, as some of the best the Alpine Lakes Wilderness offers appears only on the map.

From the beginning, the journey was a labor of love. I had succumbed quickly, effortlessly, to the charms of the wilderness, had invested in her all my energies and emotions. It was an intense relationship, and an innocent one. For my love was blind, an infatuation. I had seen the faults — the

highways, the resorts, the dams, the logger's axe —
yet they were not fatal flaws. Not to the eyes of the
lover.

But my eyes were turned ever outward, taking
my passion for granted, never looking inside myself. So I did not see how Washington was eating
away at my heart. How my steps had become hur-
ried, forced, trudging along a map, no longer
caressing the land. How my trail journal had become an obligation, no longer a plaything, carrying
odes to my sweet. I did not sense the hollowness
beneath my joy. I was in love, damn it, nothing
could ever be wrong. And the shadows of depression grew silently longer.

Then, near the end of my stay in the Alpine
Lakes region, I met up with Rick, my companion of
the High Sierra. He had skipped northern California, had worked for five weeks at a lakeside resort
in southern Oregon, and was then hitting a few of
the high spots in Washington before leaving the
trail. His quiet nonchalance was a stunning contrast to my hyper moodiness; next to his shiftless
mellowness, I was water droplets sizzling and pop-
ping on the ready griddle. I could ignore the niggling in my innards no longer. The next day, I
reached Stevens Pass, the last of the ski settle-
ments, and hitched down to Skykomish to pick up
my supply box and confront my emotions.

I could not get a handle on the cause of my
malady — perhaps it was a fear of the Storm King,
perhaps it was anxiety about the nearing Journey's End and the unknown that lay beyond — but
the symptoms were obvious: I was trying to escape.
Speed was an escape; I didn't have to live with
myself when I was pushing a ridgetop, straining to
make one more lake before dark. People were an

escape, for I would take myself out of the wilderness to enter the social milieu. Books were an escape; Gail Sheehy's *Passages,* bought in Portland, was the first non-trail-related book I had carried. Evenings found me entangled in the theories of mid-life crisis, ignoring the riot of color in the celebration of Sol's farewell.

I had to get back in touch. Take time to watch a tribe of Clark nutcrackers exercise an indecipherable pecking order while scavenging sardines from an open tin in a lakeside firepit. Take the time to let my emotions flow like the wild river. I mailed Sheehy back to Portland, installed a governor on my engine. The confrontation had succeeded and my deamons seemed vanquished. Despite the Storm King's return, I could hardly sleep that night with my eagerness to return to my lover.

The mountains are a carnival with the hillsides dipped in cotton candy, elves tapdancing on the shelter roof. I whisper smoke signals to the gods — I am well, but be kind — and the elves repair to the wings. I move off into the clouds, draping them from my shoulders or blowing them away like an unruly lock of hair. Sol searches out the weak spot in the Storm King's armor to send down a ray of morning. There's even an occasional chink of blue, like a penny lying lone in the gutter. But the Storm King comes to sweep clean the streets, brushing the blues away with a spray of butterfly kisses. I pitch my own chink of blue at Pear Lake. The Storm King raises his voice, spittle flying from his mouth, but I am not moved. The storm fades, clouds cracking with age; no pennies of blue this time, but bills of large denomination and Sol setting the stage for starry-eyed night.

*The moment I bite into the supposedly pit-
ted date and hear the grinding crunch, I know
the odds have caught up with me. Throughout
the journey, my timing had been perfection and
I brushed up against only the fringes of mis-
fortune. Now, as I spit out my mouthful of date
to examine the damage, I feel the fear of failure
for the first time. Tongue and compass mirror
tell the story: a lower molar is fractured, gum
to crown.*

I had set only one measurable goal for myself
prior to the start of the trek: to walk the length of
the Pacific Crest Trail in one hiking season. It was
an unobstrusive target, however, no carrot before
my donkey-nose. Perhaps this was due to the extraordinary scope of the undertaking — how does
one comprehend the notion of hiking 2500 miles;
what is there to hold in one's hand, where the
tangibility? Perhaps it got lost in the experience of
the moment — after plunging through knee-deep
snow or ripping through clinging chaparral, one
does not immediately reward oneself with the
thought, "I am 13 miles closer to Canada." Canada
was a goal only on a grimy, tattered sheet of paper
that I carried with my identification papers.

As the months of miles slipped easily by, however, I began to take the accomplishment of the
goal for granted, began building dreams of the
future on the foundation of its achievement. Then,
in one terrifying moment, I saw my future lying
crushed in the wreckage of a tooth. I had not
realized how important the gaining of the border
was to me until after its achievement was
threatened. As it happened, the fractured tooth did
not stand in the way of my completing the trail; it
became only one more incident among many, one

more anecdote to share with friends. But it was an enlightening and humbling experience. I left that moment with a somewhat firmer grasp on my humanity.

In the immediate wake of the tooth's fracture, when I was still uncertain of its effect, I sought the support and security of companionship. Tim and Tom had reappeared two evenings before and now we joined ranks. The tooth was not all that threatened the completion of the trail: the Storm King was beginning to assert himself. As I had left Stevens Pass to continue through a mountainscape similar to that of the Alpine Lakes region, the rains were an intermittent, predominantly daylight, companion. After we entered Glacier Peak Wilderness, however, the respites came less frequently. Near the end of our hike around Glacier Peak, the Storm King stepped up his offensive still further, and an afternoon was spent hiking up through the falling of six inches of snow. In Stehekin, one day beyond Glacier Peak Wilderness, there was a Crest Trail Register in the post office. Its pages were filled with praises sung to the peak. Yet in four days in its wilderness, following a trail that semigirdles the peak, clambering up and down its highly glaciated furrows and spurs, I saw the peak only once . . . and that was no more than a partial summit exposure from some 15 miles away.

Come on, Mother E, com'on now and pick 'em up! Pick 'em up now, girl, lift those skirts of your'n.

The rain ceases with the day and I wake to sky blossoms of orange and rose. But the old girl just loves to flirt; we break camp in a steady rain. Sol steals her heart and sends down a ray of hope to the walkers, but she warms only enough to send the valley fog climbing the hillsides after us. Not needing to follow switchbacks, it is soon nipping at our heels. At the ridgecrest, we leave the fog behind and enter snow country. The night's moisture has lightly powdered the neighboring ridges and the lower slopes of Kennedy Peak, an 8384-foot thorn in Glacier Peak's side; Mother E continues applying the make-up through the day. To the eye, I walk a dream of curvaceous canyon and snowswept rock; to the body, it is a raw, blustery, miserably wet path.

The Wet is an artless villain. It bludgeons me with its omnipresence and snaps my spirit onto its keychain. I drop my idle pace of the past few days, deciding to push for Stehekin on the morrow, and warmth and dryth. The rhythm now is not one of leisurely breaks and while-away conversation; leisure is not a convenient mood for this environment when packing limited food. One either sits in his tent with a bota of wine, friend, and magnetic Go board, or he beats it on down the trail.

It seems a typical Mother E come-on of a morning: greys and blues challenging each other for supremacy and old Sol refereeing the match. Today, however, the blues win the contest and Sol offers himself as the trophy. We plunge down from Suiattle Pass in six inches of new snow. Fir trees, pregnant with snowchild, sway heavily in the gilding sun. Wisps of cloud banner the surrounding peaks. The only sounds are the clicking of cameras and the joyful cries of three Children of the Trail at play.

*The sun continues throughout the day; we
must look elsewhere for deterioration. My left
ankle for instance, where something has been
torn-pulled-strained or simply worn to a fraz-
zle. I gimp the last 15 miles of the day, arriving
in Stehekin with a scary amount of swelling.
It's a race to the wire, folks, and it's anyone's
guess as to which will be left behind: the trail
or my body. A hot tub and an all-you-can-eat
dinner of home-made stew give a slight edge to
the body by evening's end.*

Stehekin is a charming hamlet, set at the
northern tip of the narrow glacial chasm that holds
46-mile Lake Chelan. A "lost civilization" in a
corner of the North Cascades, Stehekin is accessible only by boat, pontoon plane or foot. The 75
residents live in a world rarely found now outside
the almanacs gathering dust in our attics . . .
foodstuffs are bought in bulk to last six months, a
year, and ferried up from the town of Chelan at the
southern end of the fjord-like lake; deer are killed
and cured not as as supplemental delicacy but as a
staple of the diet; autos of 50's vintage stand at
dockside, used for little more than carrying folks to
a favorite trout hole along the 23-mile Stehekin
River Road, which dies at both ends.

A Park Service bus had brought us down the
road to the village. A soft bed. A final supply box.
Tent pitched in a lounge of the lodge to dry overnight. The next day, as God poured golden hon-
eybutter over his breakfast peaks, we were taxied
back to our trailhead for a final six days of walking.
Sol continued his cameo appearance for a day as
the trail passed through the outskirts of the North
Cascades National Park on its ascent of Bridge
Creek Canyon. Then the Storm King resumed his

reign. At Stevens Pass, at Stehekin, at Rainy Pass, where the new North Cascades Highway crossed our trail, we were hearing of Trailers quitting the path, losing sight of their quest in the deluge. For us, however, the serious weather was left behind at Glacier Peak; we were served no more than an ill-seasoned hash of snow and sun. The trail climbed out of a final canyon bottom to make a 30-mile ridgerun through the Pasayten Wilderness to the Canadian border. The Storm King cheered our finish, raising his curtains for our last day and a half to reveal the singular glacial sculpture for which the North Cascades are justly renowned.

The rains return in the night, the cycle of wetness begins again. My thoughts meander with the twistings of the trail, from the opulent greenery of my surroundings ... homefolks ... the snow waiting 3000 feet above me ... last evening's fire, perhaps the last of the journey. It is surprising to me how quickly my spirit moves from joy to survival at the drop of a color, from blue to grey.

The journey has come full circle. It was two years ago that the seeds were planted during a September week in these North Cascades. I want so much to be able to see the splendor that inspired me then, not the brooding cast of clouded peaks and sullen valleys. Extraordinary sculpture, but there's frost over all the windows in this museum. Come on, Storm King, turn off the spigot! I need to soar above these snowclad crags, to have Sol light my path to the border. I want so much to reach trail's end in a spirit of continuance rather than one of escape.

I wake to clearing but it's only a tease as the early morning climb lifts me into the clouds of snow country. I swear, the only folks getting views anymore are the owls. Visibility rarely exceeds a couple hundred feet and I look to the snow for stimulation. Here are tracks of rabbit and what appears to be cat. Here the few inches of new snow has drifted to knee depth on the steep north-slope switchbacks, yet leaves barren trail as we arc to southwestern exposures. Boots soaked in the damp of the first few miles of overgrown, canyon-bottom trail now frost the toes in ridgeline snow-walking. It is not hospitable country; I break only for lunch.

It is the final climb in America. The Storm King rides beside me, charioteer with his team of matched greys, black manes streaming in the wind, silver trappings gleaming. Dressed for war, he parades in celebration of recent conquests, welcoming my eyes to his kingdom. Mt. Baker, mantled in sunlight, shredded clouds in its rigging, rides high above the storm-tossed sea of ridges which stretch to the horizon. A striking scene, worn by my eyes as a laurel wreath by the victor. It is an acutely personal triumph, for only I know the game that has been played these several months. The warm, tight gut of adrenal fever leaves hardly a footprint in the trail as I top the climb. I rest awhile, and angels sit at my knee, listening to the summer tales of my spirit.

I wideawake in middlenight, rested and ready. Rustlings come from the neighboring tent. "How much longer do we have to put up with this darkness,' I call out. Pause. "Damn, my watch has stopped," Tom mutters. Pause. "Damn, no it hasn't; it's only two o'clock." We pass an hour or two singing one-liners from old rock songs at the moon, before drifting back to sleep.

We greet the day sluggishly. A frost-trimmed trail ushers us down to the famous border monument: drab, weathered monolith in small, shadowed clearing. I am curiously detached, not reading the monument's inscription, for even my eyes are in limbo. As we walk a last half-mile of highway to Manning Park's lodge, I begin to understand: piercing yowls of delight, hysterical giggles. But there remains disbelief. It is not fully clear to me yet that this is not just another supply stop.

Tom's folks had flown out from Chicago to meet him at trail's end, and I allowed myself to be gathered up by their festivities. It was a matter of self-preservation, really. I was afraid of how far I would fall once I let go of the trail; celebrating with Tim and Tom helped maintain the connection.

It was a strong connection in its own right, though. Bound by months of living together, I was Mother E's common-law husband. Re-entry into civilization would be like learning a new language, thinking first in my now-native trail-tongue before translating into city-speak. Outside of Hope, British Columbia, the road sign read: Vancouver — 100 miles. I remarked that it wouldn't take but a week to get there. We all laughed, but I wasn't sure of the joke.

Late that night, in a Vancouver hotel room, I opened my journal for one final entry:

The full moon rises, luminous, golden. A harvest moon. The journey's been six moons growing, growing in the fertile soil of a soul left city-fallow. The yield has been abundant.

Washington Trail Log

Date	Camp	Elevation	Mileage
Aug. 28	Ashes Lake	100	1
29	Panther Creek Campground	940	14
30	Tombstone Lake	4560	19
31	Trout Lake Creek	3310	22
Sept. 1	Sheep Lake	5780	15
2	Coleman Weedpatch area	5050	23
3	McCall Basin	5190	18
4	White Pass — supply pick-up	4480	11
5	Fryingpan Mt. area	4650	12
6	Tipsoo Lake Trail junction	5920	16
7	Arch Rock Shelter	5680	20
8	Blowout Mt. area	5150	18
9	Stirrup Creek area	3540	23
10	Snoqualmie Pass — supply pick-up	2880	13
11	Goldmeyer Hot Springs	1740	12
12	Waptus Lake	3040	16
13	Deception Lakes	5060	17
14	Skykomish — supply pick-up	930	15
15	Lake Janus	4150	10
16	Pear Lake	4830	9
17	Cady Ridge area	5380	10
18	Sitkum Creek	3950	17
19	Milk Creek	3800	13
20	Miners Ridge area	5550	19
21	Stehekin — supply pick-up	1120	20
22	Hide-Away Camp	3500*	13
23	Porcupine Creek	5080	8
24	Brush Creek	4600*	18
25	Tamarack Peak area	6600*	17
26	Hopkins Lake	6170	18
27	Manning Park, B. C.	3800	15

Totals
472 miles
31 hiking days

*elevation approximate to the nearest 100 feet

Journey totals
2464 miles
162 hiking days
15 layover days

Afterword

The question was invariably asked, usually in parting: "Would you do it again?" they would ask. I would grin, "No one ever does this twice." Engagingly flip. They would laugh and turn to go. I never gave it a second thought. Then I met Bill Foster on the slopes of Mt. Hood. He used the same words, but somehow it was a different question. I could not respond; I did not know the answer.

Perhaps the problem was that I did not really know the question. What was it that I was doing that I should want to do again? I thought back to the origins of the journey, to that moment of exhilaration so keen that it took my breath away, when I felt perfectly placed in space and time. I wanted to live that experience forever, to capture it and keep it by me like a manservant. I thought that to recreate the environment would recreate the experience and so had gone for a long walk in the mountains. And it had worked. Day after day, I would pause to find that the exquisite feeling had crept up on me while I'd had my back turned. But it was a fleeting moment, no more substantial than an angel's breath. When I would try to focus, it would flit away, like the amoeboid image of a dust particle on the surface of the eye that always stays one glance ahead of your gaze. So I would bed down each night, looking forward to the next day, wondering where I would next meet the moment of unadulterated joy.

Somewhere in Washington, I began to realize that the trail was going to end one day and, with it, the magic I had found there. It was just a superficial understanding at first; I saw the numbers in the trail guide getting smaller. Then late one afternoon, on the first day out of Stehekin, I met a couple hiking south. They had started in Canada only short days earlier, were heading south on foot, then snowshoe, then cross-country ski, for another two or three months. As we went our separate ways, a vague, faintly discomforting feeling came over me which I couldn't quite identify. And then I had it ... envy. I envied this couple their three months when I had but five days remaining. For they would be continuing their search for the divine moment, while I would be ... where?

Then I knew the answer to the question.

Menu

The menu is easily the most idiosyncratic of the concerns of the backpacker, regardless of the duration of the trip. I met a fellow who ate his freeze-dried dinners uncooked and unreconstituted, and another who subsisted largely on peanut butter and crackers. Although I subscribe to the axiom that if it doesn't taste good, you won't eat it, on a long-distance hike there are some concerns that take a higher priority than taste appeal.

The first is carbohydrates. Although I grant the importance of protein for cell regeneration, and fat for fat-soluble vitamin transport, it is carbohydrates that move you down the trail. It is impossible to plan for too many carbohydrates in your trail diet. My breakfast, snack and lunch menu was virtually all carbos — my pre-trip pantry included neary 90 pounds of granola and over 130 pounds of dried fruit — yet every one-horse market would see me hitting up a quick fix of 2-3000 calories of sugar and starch.

Calories are something else that will undoubtedly get short shrift in your menu planning, perhaps because of a tendency backpackers have to plan diets with pack weight as the prime consideration. Weight loss, and strength loss, due to insufficient fuel may be a minor issue on a short trip, but it is of considerably greater significance over several weeks or months. The National Outdoor Leadership School allots 3750 calories a day on their activities, but not even that amount would have helped the young fellow I met who lost 75 pounds on his Crest Trail trek. To aid the transition to my trail diet, I had gained 10 pounds prior to my venture. I had provided for a seemingly excessive 3500 calories a day, with a reasonable coverage of fat, protein and carbohydrates. Yet within three weeks I had lost that 10 pounds, and was plagued by a feeling of running-on-empty for the remainder of the journey.

Another consideration that is easily overlooked is vitamin and mineral needs. I know this is going to sound like your mother talking, but I think a vitamin/mineral supplement is indispensable. Hiking a daily 10-20 miles for weeks on end is an extremely stressful activity, with both physical and emotional impact. Yet, at this time when your body's demands for vitamins and minerals are escalating, your intake of vitamin-rich fresh foods, especially fruits and vegetables, is limited. I included a high-potency multi-vitamin and additional mineral supplement in my menu planning, to which I credit my trek's being free of flu, colds, emotional depression and similar lowered-resistance ailments to which many Crest Trailers fell victim.

One final suggestion for after you've procured all your food supplies: break them down into daily packages, particularly your snack foods. Weight considerations will prevent you from carrying all the food demanded by your rigors, and if you rely on day-to-day rationing of that four-pound bag of gorp, you can expect to overeat at the beginning of a supply leg and starve at its end.

What follows is an annotated description of my Crest Trail menu: what I used, what worked and what changes I made as the journey progressed.

Breakfast:

    cold: 4 oz. granola
              1 oz. raisins
              1 oz. powdered milk

    hot: 2 oz. Roman Meal instant cereal
              1 oz. raisins
              1 oz. powdered milk
              honey

The granola breakfast was used for nearly all of the trip, hot cereal being planned only for the Weldon-to-Yosemite leg of the Sierra Nevada and the last two weeks of Washington, when I thought the likelihood of cold weather warranted a hot breakfast. Although Roman

Meal makes the finest of the commercial hot cereals to my taste — non-mushy texture and distinctive taste due to its use of several grains — I found that I enjoyed my granola more; it was tastier and stayed with me longer into the day.

I say *my* granola because I made it, nearly 90 pounds of it for breakfast and snack bags. I was elbow-deep, mixing wet and dry ingredients in kitchen wastebaskets and perfuming/stinking up the house (depending on whether you asked me or my housemates) for several days. Consumer-group studies indicate that many commercial granolas won't even keep crabgrass alive; substituting "natural" honey for the "unnatural" refined sugar used in other commercial cereals, they are just another sweet food (which is, however, a favorable recommendation for the long-distance hiker, whose needs are for food to keep him/her going rather than food to keep him/her healthy). By making my own granola, I was able to alter the ingredients to meet my needs. For example, the recipe for my breakfast granola had large amounts of different nuts, seeds and soybeans to complement the protein in the milk. But for motoring through the day, I wanted carbohydrates, so I eliminated virtually all the nuts and seeds from the snack granola recipe.

Lunch/Snack:
> ¾ pound bag of granola and mixed dried fruit, about half of each
> 1 Wilson bacon bar
> ½ package Knorr or Maggi dried soup
> alfalfa sprouts

The granola/fruit bag and bacon bar were daily staples throughout the trip. I never tired of them, found them always to be tasty and satisfying, although not entirely filling. The bacon bar is an expensive investment (even at discount they cost me $1.75 apiece), but one three-ounce bar filled my entire fat and nearly my entire protein requirement, replenished salt lost to perspiration, and provided several hundred calories. If I had it to do over again, I would probably forego the bacon bars in exchange for less expensive and more greatly needed carbohydrate foods.

My choice of dried fruit — figs, pitted dates, prunes, apples, pears — was primarily a function of personal taste, except in the case of the prunes. Not only are prunes one of the least expensive dried fruits, but I find sucking on the pit while I'm walking keeps my mouth sweet and moist.

The dried soups and alfalfa sprouts were included to provide variety in my diet. I dropped them from the menu when I carried the 22-day supply of food into the High Sierra, because they didn't provide enough calories to justify their weight and space. Besides, the Knorr and Maggi soups are not instant and require as much fuel as dinner and breakfast foods combined (instant soups such as Lipton's and Nestle's are so tasteless I wouldn't consider them regardless of the duration of the trip, and backpacking food manufacturers' products are grossly overpriced). By summer, it was too hot for soup and too difficult to find the fine line between wilting and rotting in sprouting the alfalfa seeds. In more temperate conditions, I got crisp, healthy sprouts in about five days by keeping them in a plastic water bottle with a cheesecloth top and rinsing them twice a day.

Dinner:
> Richmoor or Mountain House freeze-dried dinner, with two ounces textured vegetable protein (TVP) or a Wilson bar added
> whole dried banana/instant pudding
> tea and honey

Having indulged good taste at the expense of light weight with my breakfasts and snacks, I reversed my priorities and used freeze-dried dinners in the evenings. Richmoor and Mountain House were, at that time, the only makers of instant, just-add-boiling-water, backpacking dinners. Not having used them before, I spent a full month kitchen-testing selected dinners to find the most tolerable, eventually using about a dozen varieties. The TVP, aside from adding protein and calories, provided considerable extra bulk; it was nice to feel full and sated at least once a day. The meat bars were used only during the High Sierra leg, when I thought their extra fat would aid in combating the cold of high altitude and winter snowpack.

Whole dried bananas are a natural-food-store delicacy, and the least expensive dried fruit. The half-pound package of eight bananas was just about perfect to cover desserts for each 7-10 day supply leg . . . at first! Halfway through Oregon, however, I finally faced up to the fact that I was forever rapaciously devouring my entire dessert supply on the first evening after a pick-up, and started supplementing the bananas with a package of instant pudding each evening.

For me, tea with honey is a mark of a leisurely and contemplative experience. If it had not been dropped from the menu due to the hot weather of early summer, it would surely have fallen victim to the general ambience of continual movement.

Equipment

Food may be what Crest Trailers talk about when they dream of home or are preparing some vile, freeze-dried concoction, but equipment is what they talk about even when their belly's full and their taste buds delighted. It is a diverse crowd that gathers at the Mexican border in the spring and the only common denominator, it seems, is what is carried on their backs. What do you say after you say "Hello?" . . . why, you say "Hey, how do you like your Trail Wedge tent?" For the first several weeks of the trip, Trailers catching up to and meeting me for the first time would exclaim "Oh, you're the guy with the Backmagic pack. I've heard about you. Hey, how do you like it anyway?"

So, for the last time, here is how I liked my Backmagic pack, and everything else I carried at one time or another along the way.

Packs

North Face Backmagic frame pack
Hine Snowbridge fanny pack

There has long been support for the concept of a mechanism that allows the hipbelt to move with the hips, independent of its connection with the rest of the pack, thus eliminating the torque across the hiker's back which is created by the hips and shoulders moving in opposition to each other. However, when The North Face brought out its Backmagic pack in late 1976, there was a great deal of skepticism about the durability of the flexible plastic piece in its hipbelt assembly. My experience with the Backmagic, after 2500 miles and carrying weights of up to 85 pounds, was that it was a supremely comfortable, spacious and sturdy pack. And while I heard countless stories of pack breakdowns, the only flaw in the Backmagic was one seam in the hipbelt beginning to come undone at journey's end.

I reversed the fanny pack and used it as a bellypack in conjunction with the frame pack. Into the belly pack went guidebook, maps and compass, camera, chapstick, hat, gloves, bandanna, notebook and pens, and any other small equipment that I might have wanted to reach without unharnessing completely. It was a very effective and practical system.

Sleeping gear

Snowlion Ultralight down bag
blue foam pad, ¾ length
Jan Sport Trail Wedge tent

I chose a down bag rather than a synthetic for its light weight and compactness, and hoped that the weather would not severely test my ability to keep it dry. With the exception of my stupidity in trying to outguess the weather at Yosemite's Donohue Pass, and with the aid of a drought year, I succeeded, although the extreme atmospheric humidity of the rain and snow in Washington tended to appreciably diminish the loft. My only criticism of the Ultralight bag was that the hood was not large enough. And of course, with two pounds of down, it was too warm during the summer months; however, unless you have a summer bag you can exchange your heavier weight bag with, undue summer warmth is the price you pay for the security of sufficient warmth in snow country.

I include the tent with my sleeping gear since, with one exception, that was the purpose for which it was used. Actually, I found it more valuable in protecting me from the evening mosquitoes than as shelter from the storm. The one instance when I needed it for more than sleep — to sit out the Mothers Day snowstorm in the Piute Mountains — was argument enough for carrying a full-size, full-shelter tent, rather than a tube tent, bivouac bag, or the like. Sitting out a storm, particularly if you are alone, is when a sense of security becomes of paramount importance; being straitjacketed in a bivvy bag or doused from either end of a tube tent brings you little peace of mind.

Like most two-person tents, the Jan Sport Trail Wedge is best used as a one-person shelter, although its semidome shape is a creative use of space, allowing great maneuverability within. It stood firm in winds up to 40 mph, belying its seeming fragility. My main criticism of the 1976 model I used was that the system for guying the rainfly was insufficient for keeping it from contacting the tent body and thus wetting the non-waterproof tent body with the condensation on the underside of the fly.

Footwear

Danner boots: **Model 6490, a lightweight trail shoe**

a prototype, heavier weight, off-trail-type hiking boot

running shoes
Polarguard booties
wool liner socks
wool ragg outer socks

The lightweight hiking shoes were my main footwear. I logged some 1700 miles in them, getting them resoled after 1300 miles. I used the heavier weight boots for the snow and rock of the Sierra Nevada, between Weldon and Lake Tahoe, and again in northern Oregon while my 6490s were being resoled. Unlike the Trailer who carried two pairs of boots with him right from the start because he had heard he would wear one pair out in the course of the trip, I shuttled my boots back and forth via my supply boxes.

My 6490s were so comfortable I thought I could dispense with the added weight of separate camp shoes. However, no boot is comfortable after a full day's hiking

and I greeted my Weldon supply box, with its Polarguard booties, with unremitting joy. I used the booties
for the Sierra snow country and again in northern
Washington. The booties were great for sitting around
camp, but walking up a snowbank from the evening
creek was almost as much work as the entire day's
walking, because they give the foot no support what-
soever. At the summer solstice the booties were exchanged for running shoes. The running shoes were not
only soothing to evening feet, but were pressed into
service also for some of the long days of roadwalking in
northern California, for they gave me more cushion than
my boots.

I carried three pairs of wool liner socks and three pair
of wool outer socks at a time, exchanging them for three
new pairs of each every 5-6 weeks. None ever wore out,
but the greater cushion of the new socks was deeply
appreciated. The conventional arguments for the
double-sock method are that it creates less friction
against the foot and it wicks moisture away from the foot
more quickly than if a single sock is worn; the chance of
blistering is thus decreased. In addition, there is greater
insulating value with this "layer method." More important for the long-distance hiker, however, is that by
fitting your boots for two socks, you can remove one pair
to compensate for the slight swelling that will occur in
your feet toward the end of a long day. The one time I got
a blister, on the outside of a little toe in the first week of
the trek, removing the liner sock allowed it enough room
to relieve the pressure and aggravation after moleskin
and bandages had failed.

Clothing

fishnet wool longjohns
fishnet wool t-shirt
cotton t-shirt
nylon running shorts
army surplus lightweight wool pants
longsleeve wool shirt

nylon windbreaker
rain pants
high gaiters
mountain parka
down parka
poncho
bandannas
white, wide brim tennis hat
wool balaclava
army surplus wool liner gloves
ski mitts

In the city, I like cotton. In the mountains, I believe in wool. The hype about wool is that its natural oils and thick pile repel moisture somewhat and it retains its density to keep you warm even after it's soaked through. All of which is sufficiently true for me to usually carry at least one layer of wool for my entire body, regardless of the season. Cotton — as in the jeans, cut-offs and t-shirts that seem to be standard backpacker dress, particularly during the summer — absorbs moisture immediately and dries out only slowly under the best of conditions. When you consider that a wet body chills at a rate up to 24 times greater than a dry body, and you think of the high winds and fickle weather that frequent the mountains, the preponderance of cotton in our mountain wardrobes appears a foolhardy practice at best. However, you should not think that you can waltz through the rain in your wools without a care in the world; once you are soaked through, you would need completely airtight garments to avoid the chilling effect of moving air on dampened body.

I carried a cotton t-shirt as a luxury, a clean garment to wear in towns and on warm evenings in camp. For me, cotton's response to moisture works against it in warm weather conditions also. I sweat profusely and don't want the unpleasantness of wearing a damp, clammy t-shirt and shorts through the day, or having to carry a closetful of dry changes. Nylon is quick-drying; in using nylon running shorts, and a nylon windshell when I wanted a top, I could be drenched with sweat, take a 15-minute break, and start walking again in dry clothes. What's more, the theory that mosquitos are repelled by bright colors — yellow, orange, red — and attracted to dark colors — green, brown, blue — seemed to hold true: I received maybe a half dozen bites through my red windbreaker during the entire trip, although I never applied repellent to it or my torso.

There are a number of ways of dealing with the problem of staying dry in a rainstorm. I use a poncho, since the amount of heat I generate necessitates the greater heat-dissipating air circulation that a poncho provides, as compared to any other sort of waterproof garment. I used a length of nylon cord as a makeshift sash to minimize the poncho's flapping in the wind. This setup was a bit tedious when I wanted to take a break, however, what with all the untying and unsnapping and then trying to get the poncho on straight again over a high-loaded pack. The rain pants were probably the one piece of clothing I least needed; I found them to be too warm in their waterproofness and too confining to my movement. I have always found pants to limit my freedom of movement so, in all but the most extreme conditions of snow and cold, have hiked in my shorts and high gaiters, keeping wool pants dry in the pack for the warmth needed in evening camp.

By June, I was sending the cold-weather clothes home. All the wool underclothes, the down parka, the mountain parka, rain pants, and ski mitts. I also sent my wool gloves and balaclava home from Lake Tahoe, a move I regretted two weeks later when there were near-freezing temperatures in the Mt. Lassen area in early July.

I am a great believer in sun hats. I have to be, as my hair is thinning and my scalp would scorch easily in the increased ultraviolet radiation from the sun at high altitudes. However, beneath the shade of a wide brim and the heat-reflective nature of the white color, I feel appreciably cooler wearing the tennis hat than going bare-headed. Too, I don't have to worry about sweating all the sunscreen off my forehead and nose, leaving them open to burning, when I am in the shade of the hat.

Cookwear

EFI LP-gas cartridge stove
Optimus 731 LP-gas cartridge stove
two-quart aluminum cookpot
Sierra cup
spoon
Gerry tubes (for honey)
wood matches
paper matches
fire starters
quart water bottles
1½ gallon collapsible plastic water jug

I've put the stoves at the top of the list so I can get my major equipment beef out of the way: the only piece of equipment that I was really thoroughly dissatisfied with at journey's end was my stove. When I began backpacking eight years ago, I bought a Bleuet stove because the gas cartridges looked to be less trouble to deal with than a white-gas stove, which needed to be filled and primed. Inertia and the attractiveness of the collapsibility of the EFI stove (first marketed and more widely known as the Gerry Mini) resulted in my switching to an LP-gas cartridge stove when my Bleuet began to fade.

Being able to remove the self-sealing cartridge on an LP-gas stove is a big advantage in efficient packing, but it also works against you in keeping the stove functioning. Butane and LP gas are very clean-burning fuels; their stoves rarely come with any means for unclogging them, since clogging should not happen. However, LP gas is a fuel of such fine consistency that the orifice through which the fuel passes can be designed smaller than the orifice in, for instance, a white-gas stove. When you remove the cartridge, you expose the tiny, uncleanable orifice to dust, pollen and the like. My EFI clogged about three days into the High Sierra leg of the trail; what with the extra cartridges I was carrying to melt snow for water if need be, I had to carry the dead weight of a stove and six cartridges for nearly three weeks. At The Cornice in Mammoth Lakes, owner Ed replaced the clogged orifice for free; the new one clogged five days later. I had so many LP gas cartridges stockpiled at home that, when I called for a new stove, I had another LP-gas model sent. The Optimus got me through the rest of the trip, but I no longer trust LP-gas cartridge products. I can't recommend any other stove — I'm still trying to work my way through all the leftover gas cartridges from my PCT trip — but I definitely don't recommend the LP-gas stoves.

When the stove was on the fritz, I cooked over small stick fires (or traveled with others), using wood hardly bigger than a lead pencil. Although I needed my homemade fire starters only once, they gave me a much-needed sense of security. They were simply squares of wax-impregnated cotton cloth, made by dipping a pillow case or similar thin cotton material, into a melted mixture of paraffin (two parts) and beeswax (one part). Use an old ruler to smooth out the cloth and wipe off the excess wax, then let dry. I cut them into 3″ x 4″ squares for carrying, then into strips for use. To use, drape two or three stripes over your tinder and small twigs, and another couple strips at the top of a teepee formation of slightly larger sticks. The bottom firestarters will burn hot for 3-5 minutes as a rule and the upper strips will burn more slowly, dripping melted wax to feed your fledgling fire. They are cheap and effective.

Accessories

Swiss army knife
first-aid kit
whistle
Mallory flashlight
50 feet nylon cord
toilet paper
sunglasses

sunscreen
chapstick
Sportsmate II mosquito repellent
mosquito headnet
notebook and pens
hiking staff
crampons

Accessories are accessories; the list is about the same for everyone, give or take a few items. I carried crampons between Weldon and Tuolumne Meadows after a hazardous early-morning descent on the crusty snow above Mt. San Jacinto's Fuller Ridge made me want a bit more security for descending the north side of the high passes in the Sierra. However, I never used them. You are more likely to benefit from snowshoes than crampons but, unless it has been an exceptionally heavy snow year, the snowshoes will spend more time weighing down your pack than aiding your movement.

My hiking staff, however, handcarved from ash by a friend, was indispensable. It lent rhythm to my pace and security to my boulder fords of early-season streams. I even used it, somewhat clumsily, in place of an ice axe for climbing Mt. Whitney.

The mosquito headnet was carried in memory of a bad mosquito experience on the Tahoe-Yosemite Trail the previous time I had been in the Sierra, several years before. This time, I sent it back home from Lake Tahoe, never having used it, though my relatively gentle treatment at the hands of the mosquitos may have been due in part to the effects of the drought year. I mention the brand of mosquito repellent I used for the benefit of all members of the Cutters cult: Sportsmate II has the same active ingredient as Cutters but about double the concentration.

Routefinding

Silva compass
USGS topographic maps
Forest Service recreational maps
Wilderness Press trail guides

Equipment

The PCT is admirably described in the Wilderness Press guides. However, there are sections of the route which are a melange of trail bits, overgrown jeep paths, and logging roads, which can change dramatically from one year to the next as new sections of permanent trail are constructed. I found myself doing map and compass work in areas where I had not expected any routefinding difficulties, and soon learned that I needed to pay attention to trail directions and personal location as an ongoing process, rather than just at those times that the trail guide alerted me to potential problems.

I found it very helpful to write the various national forests and get word of recent and anticipated trail changes. Even with the latest information, however, you should be prepared for the inevitable temporary detours with their even more temporary markings. The national-forest recreational maps are surprisingly useful; though nondetailed, they give you a broad perspective and are especially helpful for planning escape routes in bad weather.

I carried USGS topographic maps for the San Jacinto Wilderness, the San Bernardinos and San Gabriels, the Sierra Nevada between Weldon and Lake Tahoe, and northern Washington. I carried them for any area that I thought might be snow-covered, thus necessitating map and compass work, because the maps in the early editions of the California volume of the Wilderness Press trail guide were virtually illegible. Although the maps in the current editions are now quite readable and functional, I find the narrow scope of the strip maps to be somewhat disconcerting.

Camera equipment

Konica C-35, with ultraviolet/skylight filters for both black and white and color film
Kodachrome 64 color slide film
Kodak Plus-X black-and-white film
Lens paper and nonfogging fluid cleaner

Though the fellow I met near Mt. Whitney carrying 45 pounds of camera equipment was well in the extreme, it is common for backpackers to unduly weigh themselves down with enough equipment to cover all eventualities. I doubt that my total kit weight ever exceeded two pounds. If I were mounting a photographic expedition, I would not undertake to hike the entire PCT in one season, and vice versa. It is a matter of setting priorities and being aware of what you are capable of accomplishing. All the perfect scenes that I came across at mid-morning, which needed early evening light to realize their perfection, I had to simply envision in my mind's eye and record it there rather than on film, because the demands of the long-distance hiker superseded the demands of the photographer.

The Konica C-35 is a small, semi-automatic camera with a built-in 38 mm, semi-wide-angle lens. It therefore has limited capabilities — no telephoto, no extreme wide angle, no macro/closeup. Within those limitations, I then set about maximizing the conditions for good photography. From a local chemical plant I bought a couple jars of silica gel in bulk. Silica gel is the desiccant that you see in small paper packets, packed in with all new electronic equipment to prohibit moisture build-up during shipping. I created my own packets, wrapping small piles of gel in Kleenex (silica gel comes in a crystalline form and is a gel in name only), and putting a couple in each resupply box. The silica gel was an aid not only in protecting the film from moisture, but also in keeping the semiperishable foods, e.g., granola and dried fruit, from fermenting during their several weeks of shipping and waiting in post offices.

The other step I took in preparation for the trek was to arrange with a small custom photo lab in my hometown to handle all my photo processing and storage of processed film. Every one of my supply boxes had a pre-addressed envelope for me to mail them my exposed film. They processed the black-and-white film themselves, making up contact sheets for the use of the newspaper for whom I was writing a series of articles. They sent the slide film to Kodak. On its return, they would put the slides in clear plastic slide sheets I had provided for them, and label each roll. On the trail, I had noted each subject and exposure number. When I returned home, it was then an easy matter to identify and sort out the several hundred slides.

Library

The Hunting Hypothesis by Robert Ardrey

Sierra Nevada Natural History by Tracy I. Storer and Robert L. Usinger

Fire and Ice: the Cascade Volcanoes by Stephen Harris

Indian Legends of the Pacific Northwest by Ella Clark

Passages by Gail Sheehy

I began the trip with the Robert Ardrey book, but only because I had been reading it on the bus and had 60 pages remaining. I didn't want to carry books, not so much because they were a dispensable weight, but because reading was cityplay, something to be done at home and, for me, often a means for removing myself from the life around me. I wanted no obstruction to the mountains, to my experience of the journey, and wondered what motivated the other Trailers to undertake the trail — those Trailers who received a new mystery or science-fiction novel in each supply box, who would remove themselves from the company and the country so as to finish their book before picking up their new supply on the morrow.

I had considered carrying a natural-history field guide of one sort or another, but had decided against it for reasons of pack weight. My High Sierra hiking companions shared with me their history and geology books, however, and I came to realize how my ignorance of natural and cultural history limited my experience of the mountains. After the one-time-only, 85-pound pack of the High Sierra, I could afford the weight of a book or two, and so bought *Sierra Nevada Natural History* in Mammoth Lakes. It was replaced by *Fire and Ice* in Ashland, Oregon, and the Indian legends book, a spontaneous purchase at Crater Lake.

I took a four-day break in Portland, after finishing the Oregon portion of the trail, and thought to carry something with which to while away the rainy hours of evening. Sheehy's *Passages* was the pop-psychology book of the year, recommended by friends. Besides, I felt myself going through a significant passage of my own. The Sheehy book was engrossing; I found myself reading it, rain or shine, to the exclusion of everything else at times. So I stayed up half the night in Skykomish to finish it in order that I could send it away and return to the mountains undistracted.

Appendix C

Special Logistical Considerations

Through my journey, I was struck by the whimsy and innocence that seemed to guide so many of my fellow-trekkers: the 100-pound pack, the 25-mile-per-day pace, the summery wardrobe that took no account of the mountain's potential for winter in July. If you are entertaining the notion of a PCT trip, backpacking experience and simple common sense should steer you around most such misdirected practices. However, there are some considerations and logistical issues that are peculiar to marathon thinking.

Options for resupplying

There are three methods commonly used for restocking your trail larder: establishing caches at points along the trail, shopping at markets convenient to the trail, and having supplies periodically mailed to you. If you are planning to hike all or much of the PCT, then caching your supplies is not very practical. Not only does it require a great investment of time — and gas — to drive your entire route and find local people to hold your stores, but if you are planning trailside caches, you run the risk of forgetting where they are or having them looted by other travelers or, if not adequately sealed and concealed, wildlife.

Neither is buying your food as you travel a particularly efficient means of resupply, as the nearby hamlets are often no more than a fishing or ski resort, their groceries carrying little more than snack foods and canned goods. Even if you have access to a supermarket, it will be difficult to minimize your food weight since markets don't cater to backpackers' needs, and the dried goods they do offer are typically sold in greater amounts than the individual or small party can use.

The method that allows you the greatest control over what you eat is to have your supplies mailed to you, c/o general delivery. The Wilderness Press guides even identify the most accessible postal points. Mailing your supplies also allows you greater choice in meeting your other equipment needs. And if your pre-trip planning has been off the mark — and it will be — you can mail unwanted gear on to a more suitable supply point.

Be sure to write each of your mail drops in advance of your trip to inquire about accepted practice. The Postal Service is only required to hold general delivery mail for 15 days, but many a backwater post office will keep your package for several weeks. Just make sure to have it mailed 3-4 weeks ahead of your expected pick-up date. Your scheduling can be affected, too, by whether the post office has weekend hours or limited daily hours. Since many mountain communities have only seasonal postal delivery, you will want to find out when their season begins; if you arrive at Yosemite's Tuolumne Meadows before the second week in June, for instance, you will find your package is being held in Yosemite Valley, a 60-mile hitchhike away.

Pack weight

The number of Trailers laboring under packs of 80 or 90 pounds was legion. I'm not sure if the idea of hiking from Mexico to Canada is so fraught with *macho* undertones that it requires a *macho* pack of such weight, or if it is simply a matter of haphazard planning, but there is little reason and far less pleasure in carrying such a burden.

To cut your load down to size, use every resupply stop available, for food weight is your greatest variable. Choose clothing and equipment that can meet multiple needs. Be selective in what "non-essential" items you carry — e.g., fishing equipment, cameras, natural-history field guides, town clothes, etc.

Pace

The basic factors are, of course, what physical condition you are in and how closely you want to be able to view your surroundings. If you are attempting to complete the entire PCT in one hiking season, then the parameters set by the extended winter season in the mountains will dictate a pace of 15 miles or more a day. But don't forget to consider that you have about 3½ hours more daylight to play with at the summer solstice than at either equinox. And that your pack weight fluctuates widely between food-supply stops. I was surprised by the number of Trailers whose plans did not distinguish between roadwalking and slogging over the high passes of the Sierra Nevada through the remains of the winter's snowpack. No matter what pace you set for yourself at the outset, you will find that the norms set by your past experience will be amended by your marathon experience.

Company

Whether to hike solo or in company with others is a decision that usually makes itself, with custom, security, and the availability of companions shaping the decision. As with many other facets of a backcountry trip, however, the conditions of a long-distance hike complicate matters. It is difficult to strike a balance between being a member of a group and remaining an individual. This may be a minimal concern on a weekend trip, but not even in marriage are the partners expected to spend 24 hours a day with each other for several weeks at a time. And there is no arguing that the decision-making process in a group requires a finer touch than acting on your own. Take some time with your partners before you begin your trip, to share your expectations of how the group will work together, what each person wants from the experience, your needs for alone-time, and the like.

Routefinding

A commonly used hedge against routefinding difficulties is to purchase the USGS topographic maps of the trail area. However, there are several deficiencies in these USGS maps. The most obvious is that, with new

trail being constructed each year, a 1955 topo map can
be woefully incomplete. Even in cases where the PCT
follows a route shown on the map, these trails undergo
occasional rerouting, old trail junctions may no longer
exist due to side trail abandonment, and new trails and
roads are likely to have been created. Worse yet, we tend
to look at these incredibly detailed maps and take their
information as the gospel . . . it ain't necessarily so.
Based primarily on aerial photographs, topo maps can
be particularly misleading in areas of heavy forest cover,
where they omit ill-defined watercourses and misrepre-
sent the location of stream crossings and, more often, the
location of manmade objects, such as cabins and boundary signs and even trail junctions.

The most serious drawback to the topographic maps,
however, is the way in which we generally use them. We
give the map little attention until we are needing to
locate ourselves, and then no longer have a readily
identifiable frame of reference for reading the map. The
time-distance equation for measuring ground covered is
not reliable since it is a rare backpacker who has a
sufficiently well-developed sense of pace. And those
two easily located landmarks the instruction books use
for triangulation are never around when you need them
Moreover, few of us have ever had to depend on our
mapreading skills.

To better prepare yourself for using topo maps, take
part in an orienteering meet or two prior to your trip (if
you are not aware of such activities in your area, the
ROTC program at the nearest university will likely have
the information). There is no better activity for bolster-
ing your confidence, or letting you know how dismally
inadequate are your mapping skills, a much more palatable lesson when you aren't under 50 pounds of pack
with night and a stormfront closing in. Then, once on
the trail, use your maps in an ongoing process to maintain a reasonable surety of your location. For even the
most obviously marked trail can become a maze for the
inattentive.

An additional issue, particularly for hikers attempting the entire PCT, is whether to hike north to south or south to north. To minimize the effects of the preceding winter, in terms of both snowpack and weather instability, it makes the most sense to start in the south and follow the spring season north. Too, the Wilderness Press trail guides are written south to north.

Physical conditioning

The physical stress of hiking day in and day out, oftentimes long miles, is incomprehensible; there is no way to adequately prepare yourself for it. As the saying goes, "the best conditioning for backpacking is backpacking," but the winter months preceding a long trek don't always allow it. There are various in-city conditioning activities, however, that will help ease the eventual load. You will want to increase your cardiovascular efficiency by such aerobic activities as walking, running, swimming, bicycling and cross-country skiing. The hill-climbing muscles in your legs can be strengthened by running hills or, even better, biking and skiing long, gentle inclines. I walked around town in an old frame pack filled with firewood to get hips and shoulders used to carrying weight, but that practice grows stale quickly. Foot skin can be toughened by applying rubbing alcohol at least once a day for several weeks. Yoga and similar stretching exercises are very useful for increasing the elasticity in the muscles, though stretching during the hike itself is of even greater importance; I quit stretching after my trip began and now, 1½ years later, I am still working out the kinks.

Mental preparation

Flushed with anticipation of your journey, it is easy to immerse yourself completely in topo maps and equipment catalogues. Yet the marathon hiker is as likely to abandon the trail because s/he is "burnt out" or "it just isn't what I want to do" as s/he is because the boots don't fit just right or the tent didn't keep out the rain sufficiently.

What is motivating you? What are you wanting to accomplish on the journey? What aspects of the experience are important to you? These are especially critical questions if you have the completion of the entire PCT as your goal. When daily mileage requirements are consistently in the 12-20 mile range, gaining the end and enjoying the means rarely go hand-in-hand.

If completing the entire trail is your highest priority, look for ways of melding the process with the product once you begin your trip. I found keeping a trail journal greatly helped me to look more closely at my experience. A well-selected natural-history field guide will bring you that much closer to your surroundings. Rest days provide as refreshing a break for the mind as they do for the body. Varying your companions also provides a change of routine. Above all else, allow yourself the flexibility to alter your goals in mid-trip. For there is no drudgery as acute as hiking for several weeks after the thrill is gone.

Index

Acton 18, 23
Adams, Mt. 100-101, 102, 103
Aloha, Lake 59
Alpine Lakes Wilderness 105, 106, 107, 108, 111
American River 53
Angeles Crest Highway 12
Ant Canyon 43
Anza 21, 23
Anza Valley 3, 5
Appalachian Trail 95
Arch Rock Shelter 117
Arrowhead, Lake 12
Ashes Lake 117
Ashland 81, 82, 97, 138

backpack 126, 127, 140
Baden-Powell, Mt. 12
Baja California 3
Baker, Mt. 82, 115
Bald Mountain 97
Bear Lake 53
Beaver Dam Creek 97
Benson Lake 47, 59
Big Bear City 23, 54
Big Bear Lake 11, 12
Big Ridge 79
Black Mountain 75
Blowout Mountain 117
Blue Lakes 59
books 10-11, 39, 82, 137-138
Bridge Creek 113
Bridge of the Gods 99
Bridger, Jim 70
Brush Creek (Kern River) 43
Brush Creek (North Cascades) 117
Bubbs Creek 43
Bull Gap 79
Bull Run Creek 26, 43
Bullion Basin 104
Butterbredt Peak 19
Burney Falls 63, 79

Cabin Creek 79
Cady Ridge 117
Cahuilla Indian Reservation 21
Cajon Canyon 12, 15
Cal Tech Peak 33
Campo 2, 95
Canada 114, 116, 120
Carbon Glacier 105
Carson, Kit 70
Carson Pass 50
Cascade Range x-xi, 2-3, 49, 56, 59, 62, 65, 66, 77, 82, 83, 103-104
Castle Crags 65, 69, 79
Cathedral Peak 71

Cave Campground 79
Challenger Glacier ix
Charlton Lake 89, 97
Chelan 113
Chelan, Lake 113
Cinco 23
Cliff Lake 97
Coffee Creek 79
Coleman Weedpatch 117
Columbia River 94, 95, 96, 99
Cook and Green Pass 79
Crabtree Ranger Station 43
Crater Lake 83, 84, 85, 86, 97, 138
Crater Lake National Park 83, 97

Deadman Lake 23
Deception Lakes 117
Deer Creek 79
Deer Lake 55
Deer Springs Trail Camp 9
Desolation Wilderness 51
Devils Peak (Oregon Cascades) 85, 97
Devil's Peak (Siskiyou Mtns.) 77
Devils Postpile Natl. Monument 39, 40
Diamond Mesa 33
Diamond Peak 86, 88, 89
Donohue Pass 40, 41, 42, 43, 58, 127
Donomore Meadows 79
Dorothy Lake Pass 49
Dry Meadow 97
Duck Pass 34, 43
Dunsmuir 65, 79

Eagle Creek 94, 96
Ebbetts Pass 50

Falls Creek 59
Feather River 56, 57, 58, 59
Fish Lake 84
Five Lakes Creek 59
Forester Pass 33, 34, 50
Fork Springs 23
Forks of the Kern 43
Four Mile Lake 84
Freye Lake 97
Fryingpan Mountain 117
Fuller Ridge 134

Garfield Peak 86
General Creek 59
Geringer Grade 23
Glacier Peak 111, 112, 114
Glacier Peak Wilderness 111
Goat Rocks 102, 103
Goldmeyer Hot Springs 117

146

Index

Grass Lake 59
Grasshopper Flat 43
Grassy Hollow Campground 23
Grider Creek 76
Guitar Lake 43
Gurnsey Creek Campground 79
Hartman Bar 58, 59
Haskins Valley 59
Hat Creek Valley 63
Helen, Lake 70
Hide-Away Camp 117
Holcomb Trail Camp 23
Holcomb Valley 23
Hood, Mt. 52, 82, 83, 86, 93, 101, 119
Hope, B.C. 116
Hopkins Lake 117
Horsemen's Group Camp 23
Horsethief Canyon 23
Humboldt Summit 79
Hurley Flat 23

Ice Lakes 59
Iron Canyon Res. 63
Irvine, Mt. 32
Isabella, Lake 30
Island Lake 97

Jack Main Canyon 45
Janus, Lake 117
Jawbone Canyon 23
Jean Peak 8
Jefferson, Mt. 86, 91, 92, 93
Jefferson Park 92
John Muir Trail xi, 26, 31, 39, 43, 46-47
Jude Lake 92, 97
Jumpoff, The 75

Kelso Valley 20, 23
Kennedy Canyon 49
Kennedy Peak 112
Kern Flat 43
Kern Hot Springs 30, 43
Kern River 25, 26, 28, 30, 31, 53
Kidder Creek 79
King, Clarence 34
Kings River 43
Kitchen Creek Camp 23
Klamath River 66, 76, 77
Klickitat Canyon 102

Laguna Mountains 3
Lake of the Woods 84
Lancaster 18, 23
LaPorte 57, 59
Lassen Peak 62, 83, 131
Lassen Volcanic Natl. Park 62, 75
Leavitt Lake 49

Leavitt Meadows 50
Liebre Mountain 17
Little Jimmy Campground 23
Little Rock Creek 12, 16
logistics 139-144
Lone Pine Canyon 12, 21
Los Angeles 9, 12
Luther Mountain 84

Maidu Lake 88, 97
Mammoth Lakes 21, 34, 39, 45, 133, 138
Manning Park 116, 117
Marble Mountains 65, 66, 76, 77
Marguerette Lake 84
Marie Lake 37
Marion Mountain 8, 23
Masterson Meadow 79
Matterhorn Canyon 45
Matthieu Lakes 97
McCabe Creek 59
McCall Basin 103, 117
McCloud Reservoir 63, 64
McLoughlin, Mt. 83, 84, 85, 97
McClure Meadow 43
McRae Meadows 56
McRae Ridge 56
Meadow Lake 59
Messenger Flats 23
Mexican border xi, 2
Milk Creek 117
Miners Ridge 117
Mission Creek 9, 11
Mojave 18, 23
Mojave Desert 12, 17, 21
Mono Divide 37
Monument Peak 23
mosquitoes 48, 49, 85
Muir, John 34, 72
Muir Pass 43
Mule Bridge 79

National Outdoor Leadership School 121
Nelson Creek 79
Nicolls Peak 19
Nobel Canyon 59
North Cascades ix, 106, 113, 114
North Cascades Highway 114
North Cascades Natl. Park 113
North Fork Meadow 23
North Pickets ix

Olallie Lake 92
Old Mammoth 43
Old Sierra Highway 18, 21
Old Snowy Mountain 102
Old Station 79
Oregon Desert 83

Oregon Shakespeare Festival 82
Oregon Skyline Trail 83

Packsaddle Cave 27
Packwood Glacier 102
Palisades Creek 43
Palmdale 18, 22, 23
Palm Springs 8, 9
Panther Creek Campground 117
Paradise Park 97
Pasayten Wilderness 114
Pear Lake 109, 117
Peninsular Ranges 3
Pickhandle Point 104
Pinchot Pass 36
Piute Mountains 19, 20, 100, 127
Placer Lake 104
Porcupine Creek 117
Portland x, 7, 97, 99, 109, 138
Purple Lake 39

Rainier, Mt. 82, 83, 101, 104, 105
Rainy Pass 114
Red Butte 75
Reds Meadows 39, 43
Return Creek 59
Ritter Range 40
Rock Creek 107
Rockpile Lake 97
Rosamond 18, 23
Rosary Lakes 97
Russell Creek 91
Russian Peak 66
Ryback, Eric x

Sacramento River 63, 65, 66
St. Helens, Mt. 83, 101, 103
Sally Keyes Lakes 43
Salmon River 66, 75, 76
Salmon-Trinity Alps Wilderness 65
Salton Sea 3
San Andreas Fault 12
San Bernardino Mountains 9, 11,
   12, 13, 135
San Felipe Valley 3, 5, 23
San Gabriel Mountains 12, 17, 135
San Gorgonio Mtn. 9
San Gorgonio Pass 9
San Gorgonio Wilderness 11
San Jacinto, Mt. 8, 134
San Jacinto Mountains 8, 9, 135
San Jose Valley 3
Santiam Pass 90, 97
Sawmill Mountain 17
Scout Lake 97
Seavey Pass 47
Seiad Valley 76, 79
Selden Pass 36
Shadow Lake 43

Shale Lake 92, 97
Shasta Lake 74
Shasta, Mt. 64, 65, 69, 70, 74, 82,
   83, 84
Sheep Lake 117
Sierra Buttes 55, 56
Sierra Nevada 17, 31, 33-34, 35,
   37-38, 39, 45, 49, 53, 54, 56, 59,
   65, 100, 122, 124-25, 128 129,
   133, 134, 135, 137, 141
Silver Pass 43
Silverwood Lake 12, 14
Siskiyou Mountains 76, 77, 82
Sisters Mirror Lake 97
Sitkum Creek 117
Skykomish 108, 117, 138
Sky Lakes 83, 84
Slate Creek 59
Snoqualmie Pass 105, 106, 117
Snoqualmie River 106, 107
Snow Creek Canyon 102
Snow Lake 106
Soda Springs 43
Sonora Pass 50, 59
Sorrell Peak 19
Sourdough Gap 104
Spanish Peak 59
Stehekin 111, 112, 113, 114, 117,
   120
Stevens Pass 101, 108, 111, 114
Stirrup Creek 117
Strawberry Cienega 8
Strawberry Valley 8
Stuart Falls Camp 97
Stubblefield Canyon 45
Suiattle Pass 112
Summit Lake 97
Sunshine Shelter 97

Tahoe, Lake 21, 48, 50, 51, 59,
   101, 128, 131, 134, 135
Tahoe Natl. Forest 52
Tahoe-Yosemite Trail 45
Tahquitz Peak 7, 8, 16, 23
Tamarack Peak 117
Tehachapi Mountains 17
Thielsen, Mt. 82, 84, 87, 88, 89,
   97
Thomas Mountain 5, 7
Three-finger Jack 82
Three Points 23
Three Sisters 84, 86, 87, 88, 89,
   90, 97
Tipsoo Lake Trail 117
Toad Lake 79
Tombstone Lake 117
Tool Box Spring Camp 5, 23
Trail Creek Campground 79

Trinity Alps 65, 66, 70, 74
Trout Lake Creek 117
Trout Meadow 28
Truckee River, Upper 51, 59
Tunnel 2 Ridge 23
Tuolumne Meadows 35, 41, 42,
  43, 45, 46, 71, 134, 140
Twin Lakes 23
Tyndall Creek 33, 43

Vancouver, B.C. 116
Vidette Meadows 35, 36
Virginia Canyon 45

Wahtum Lake 96, 97
Waldo Lake 89
Walker Creek 97
Walker Meadows 49
Walker River 59
Wallace Creek 31, 32, 35, 43
Waptus Lake 117
Warm Springs River 97

Warner Springs 3, 5, 23
Warner Valley Campground 79
Washington, Mt. 82, 86
Watchman, the 86, 87, 97
Weldon 20, 23, 25, 26, 27, 39, 50,
  52, 54, 122, 128, 129, 134, 135
Whatcom Pass ix
White Canyon 50, 59
White Pass 101, 103, 104, 117
Whitewater Canyon 9, 23
Whitney, Mt. 31, 32, 34, 35, 40,
  43, 50, 93, 134, 136
Wild Plum Campground 59
Willamette Valley 87
Williamson, Mt. 16
Williams, Rex 59, 61
Woods Creek 43

Yelverton Shelter 102
Yosemite Natl. Park 21, 35, 40, 41,
  45, 47, 48, 49, 66, 122, 134
Yosemite Valley 42, 43, 82, 140